Highpoints

Highpoints

A Study of Melodic Peaks

Zohar Eitan

PENN

University of Pennsylvania Press

Philadelphia

Copyright © 1997 University of Pennsylvania Press
Printed in the United States of America on acid-free paper

10 9 8 7 6 5 4 3 2 1

Published by
University of Pennsylvania Press
Philadelphia, Pennsylvania 19104-6097

Library of Congress Cataloging-in-Publication Data
Eitan, Zohar, 1955–
    Highpoints : a study of melodic peaks / Zohar Eitan.
        p.   cm. — (Studies in the criticism and theory of music)
    Includes bibliographical references and index.
    ISBN 0-8122-3405-7 (alk. paper)
    1. Melodic analysis.   I. Title.   II. Series.
MT47.E4   1997
781.2′4—dc21   97-11405
                                                        CIP
                                                        MN

FOR LEONARD B. MEYER

CONTENTS

ACKNOWLEDGMENTS

This study, as readers may discern, is especially indebted to Leonard B. Meyer. Professor Meyer's works inspired many of the ideas presented here, and his advice and warm encouragement were invaluable at every stage of my work. For these, and for his patience, I am wholeheartedly grateful.

Throughout the preparation of this book I have received valuable assistance from friends and colleagues. In particular, I am grateful to Eugene Narmour for many perceptive criticisms and suggestions. Conversations with Dalia Cohen of the Hebrew University provided important stimulation during the difficult early stages of this endeavor. Many thanks go to Paul Shaman of the Wharton School for his highly significant assistance in my struggle with statistical issues. Joann Hoy's editorial assistance, and the invaluable suggestions of two anonymous readers for the University of Pennsylvania Press, have helped me turn a rather messy draft into a book. Thanks are also due to Shlomo Alkelai for his assistance in preparing musical examples.

Mellon Dissertation Fellowships, granted through the University of Pennsylvania Graduate School of Arts and Sciences, enabled me to concentrate my efforts on this work during two crucial years. Revisions of the book were supported by Tel-Aviv University's Basic Research Foundation.

Last but certainly not least, I wish to thank my best friend Iris Kovalio for her continuous love and encouragement, and for being herself.

Acknowledgment is due to Universal Edition, A.G., Vienna, for agreeing to the reprinting of excerpts from Alban Berg's *Lulu*, *Lyrische Suite*, and *Der Wein*.

CHAPTER 1

Why Study Melodic Peaks?

In recent years melodic contour—the shape of melodic line, as defined by registral (up/down) rather than intervallic relations—has become an increasingly important concern of music theorists, music psychologists, and ethnomusicologists. Influential theories of melody (particularly Eugene Narmour's implication-realization model, 1990, 1992) view registral direction as a defining feature of basic melodic structure;[1] students of post-tonal music (Friedmann 1985, 1987; Marvin and Laprade 1987; Morris 1987, 1993; Polansky and Bassein 1992) and ethnomusicologists (Adams 1976; Kolinsky 1965, 1966; Seeger 1960)[2] have developed formal tools for the discussion of contour features and relationships; and many psychological studies (see Dowling 1978, 1982, 1994; Edworthy 1985) have demonstrated that the importance of contour in melodic perception surpasses, under some circumstances, that of tonal and intervallic relationships.

One reason in particular makes contour an intriguing facet of melody: unlike tonal scales and the discrete, fixed intervals to which they give rise—which are specifically musical, largely learned, and culture-specific—contour is a universal facet of auditory patterning (including speech intonation and expressive vocal gestures). Correspondingly, contour perception is relatively independent of acquired schemata. This independence has been indicated by many recent psychological studies. Thus, listeners rely on contour, rather than intervals or scale-degrees, in contexts that do not require recourse to long-term memory: in the perception of novel melodies (Attneave and Olson 1971; Dowling and Fujitani 1971; Dowling 1982; Jones 1987), when retention time between compared melodies is brief (DeWitt and Crowder 1986; Dowling 1982), and in the perception of short melodies (Edworthy 1985). Furthermore, contour

---

1. Eitan 1997 discusses the role of registral direction in Narmour's model. For a different view of the function of registral direction in melodic implication see Larson 1993.

2. Statistical methods have also been used in contour analysis, particularly in the analysis of traditional and folk music. A noteworthy recent example is Huron 1996.

perception often prevails when acquired melodic schemata are not readily accessible. For instance, when recourse to tonal schemata is impractical—as when tonality is weak or when altered tunings are used—contour becomes the chief basis for the perception of melody (Dowling 1978, 1982; Watkins and Dyson 1985). Contour seems to prevail also in the melodic perception of musically unsophisticated listeners, for whom culturally acquired schemata presumably play a less important role than for trained musicians (Monahan, Kendall, and Carterette 1987; Rosner and Meyer 1986). Moreover, contour, rather than intervals or scale-degrees, is the predominant factor in infants' melodic perception (Trehub et al. 1984; Trehub 1987; Mehler et al. 1978),[3] and is an important perceptual factor in nonhuman species (Hulse et al. 1992; Weinberger and McCenna 1988).[4]

Comparative studies of speech intonation (the dimension of speech analogous to melodic contour), which demonstrate that important aspects of intonational structure are cross-linguistic (Bolinger 1986; Cruttenden 1986), also support the notion of contour as a primeval dimension of pitch information. Furthermore, studies of emotional expression in speech (Lieberman and Michaels 1962, Sedlacek and Sychra 1963) suggest that pitch contour may have cross-cultural expressive connotations, revealing that listeners, regardless of their cultural background or their ability to understand the language spoken, correctly identify the emotional mode of speech by attending to its fundamental-pitch contour.

The perception of contour thus seems to be strongly associated with psychological "nature," that is, with innate capacities and constraints. Is this primordial dimension of melody, however, still a significant structural or expressive factor in a highly stylized musical repertory, governed by complex culture-specific norms? Or do stylistic conventions and the learned constraints of pitch syntax supersede contour—its roles in aural perception and expression notwithstanding—and turn it into a structurally insignificant murmur?

My starting point in addressing this elusive issue is a simple assumption: if contour is indeed an important melodic aspect, it should have an identifiable relationship to the configuration of other musical dimensions, such as rhythm and meter, harmony, and the intervallic organization of melody. In particular, I assume that if contour is significant, conspicuous points along a melodic curve will be associated characteristically" with specific rhythmic, metric, melodic-intervallic and harmonic configurations. This book examines different repertories to explore the ways in which the most salient contoural phenomenon is associated with such configurations.

3. Trehub has shown that eight-month-old infants encode melodic contour across variations in exact pitches and intervals. Her findings may be related to developmental studies by Mehler and associates, among others, that suggest that characteristic pitch contours play an important function in an infant's response to a mother's voice, thus implying that the ability to perceive contour configurations is innate.

4. Hulse demonstrated that songbirds are sensitive to registral direction; Weinberger and McCenna revealed that sensitivity to contour originates at the neuronal level, showing that cortical neurons of cats respond to changes in contour.

A Test Case: Melodic Peaks

In music, the most conspicuous contoural phenomenon is surely that of melodic peaks, by which I simply mean the highest pitch in a melodic line. The association of peaks with salience and with expressive intensification is deeply rooted in Western musical tradition. One may recall two examples. Johann Mattheson, the prominent eighteenth-century pedagogue and theorist, distinguishes between *accent* and *emphasis*. These differ in hierarchic level and in function. In vocal music, the *accent* falls on the stressed syllable in each word, while the higher-level *emphasis* stresses the important words in the phrase; and while "The aim of accent is only the pronunciation," emphasis "points towards the emotion, and illuminates the meaning of the performance." Though melodic ascent is an important factor in both kinds of stress, it is the higher-level, emotionally loaded emphasis that "would almost always require a raising" (Mattheson 1739/1981: 370). The musical examples presented by Mattheson to illustrate his discussion clearly show his association of emphasis not merely with rise in pitch, but specifically with points of melodic culmination. For instance, in his exemplary *Arietta* (Example 1.1), A♭ — the peak pitch of the opening phrase and of the entire piece — is assigned to the word *pietosa*, to Mattheson's mind the central word in the text, and other "loaded" words (italicized in Example 1.1) serve as peaks of subsequent phrases. Peaks are thus regarded by Mattheson as creating a special, higher-level emphasis, associated with rhetorical and affective salience.

Two centuries later, while discussing music written two centuries before Mattheson's time, Renaissance scholar Knud Jeppesen stated, as one of two universal guiding principles of melodic motion, that "higher compared to deeper notes and . . . ascending in relation to descending movements . . . arouse more attention and are consequently felt to be expressive of stronger psychical activity" (Jeppesen 1927: 52).[5] As the culmination of the emphatic melodic ascent, a peak is, according to Jeppesen, a point of special importance, to be handled with a particular care in Palestrina's style. Observing how the style's ideal of a balanced, unexcited melodic motion is expressed in handling this sensitive point in the musical discourse, he points out limitations within the style on the location of peaks (rarely occur at the ends of phrases), their quantity (rarely repeated within the phrase), and their metric location (never occurring on unaccented quarter notes; see Jeppesen 1939: 83–97).

More recently, diverse theorists and analysts have associated melodic peaks with the climax of a prototypical intensity curve, usually termed the "dynamic" or "narrative" curve (see Agawu 1982, 1983, 1984, Cohen 1971, 1983; Meyer 1980, 1989; Toch 1948 for descriptions of the prototype and related analyses; Berry 1976; Cogan and Escot 1976, for relevant theoretical studies; Huron 1990a, 1990b, 1996, for statistical analyses of texture, dynamics, and melodic contour validating the dynamic curve notion). The dynamic curve is a process (which may span units of various dimensions,

5. Though Jeppesen's works deal with a specific historical style (Palestrina's), the observations cited here are meant to apply more generally.

EXAMPLE 1.1. *Arietta* from Mattheson (1739), Part II, Chapter 8, # 13.

from a phrase to an entire piece) constituting a gradual, relatively long build-up of intensity and tension (often composed of several secondary curves) up to a point or area of climax, followed by a shorter, more direct phase of abatement. The dynamic curve may describe a process of intensification and abatement in various parameters. Melodic contour, however, is often regarded as its paradigmatic representation, and its climax is frequently associated with the peak of a rising melodic line.

Like the perception of contour in general, the widely acknowledged salience of contour peaks is related to basic perceptual constraints. Recent studies in melodic perception and in speech intonation, which substantiate the importance of melodic peaks as emphatic agents and their association with heightened intensity, suggest that the source of these characteristics indeed lies beyond the field of music proper.[6] The perceptual salience of peaks seems to result from the interaction of several factors. First, a peak is a contoural "corner," a point where a change of direction takes place.[7]

6. A pitch peak is the main means of accentuating syllables in nontonal languages (Cruttenden 1986: 53). On a higher level, a high-pitch accent is commonly used to establish the intonational "nucleus" of a phrase—the part of the phrase emphasized by the speaker (note the correspondence with Mattheson's *accent* and *emphasis*). Further, a salient peak may outweigh the normative accentual structure of a phrase. The intonational nucleus is usually the last "pitch accent" (an accent created by a marked pitch change) in the phrase. This last accent need not necessarily be a peak. However, in many cases the existence of a conspicuous high pitch accent—a peak—*before* the last accent in the phrase makes this peak the nucleus (Cruttenden 1986: 49–51).

7. See Drake and Palmer 1993; Jones 1987; Monahan, Kendall, and Carterette 1987; Thomassen

Further, peaks (as well as troughs) also serve as boundary points for registral space, and are thus marked for attention (Ortmann 1926).

Why are peaks, however, more salient than troughs, which are also boundary points and contoural corners (Watkins and Dyson 1985; see also Thomassen 1982)? Though the greater salience of peaks is partly the result of the salience of higher pitches in general (Hart et al. 1990; Watson and Kelly 1981), Watkins and Dyson's experiments demonstrate that it cannot be attributed to this factor alone. The answer probably stems from another factor, whose importance in delineating the emphatic quality of peaks cannot be exaggerated: the association of pitch ascent with effort and raised tension, and the ensuing status of pitch peaks as highpoints of intensity, points of highest "energy" level. This relationship, which may account for the frequent association of melodic peaks and affective highpoints in music, is not exclusively musical. It is also prevalent in speech, where its most conspicuous expression is the cross-linguistic association [8] of intonational rise with "open," phrases, demanding continuation (such as those conveyed by implicational sentences or yes/no questions), and of fall with "closed" phrases (expressed by neutral statements, final sentences, etc; see Cruttenden 1986: 168–69).[9] Correspondingly, studies of the emotive aspects of speech intonation relate ascent in pitch with heightened, tense emotional states (O'Connor and Arnold 1961; Williams and Stevens 1972). Such relationships, as Bolinger (1985) suggests, may be iconic and kinesthetic in nature, corresponding to the association of physical ascent in space with increased effort and physiological tension.[10]

THE PRINCIPAL HYPOTHESES

The studies referred to above suggest that the emphasizing, affective, and tensional connotations of melodic peaks may represent basic, innate characteristics of human expression.[11] A study of melodic peaks can, then, serve as a test case for our initial

---

1982; Watkins and Dyson 1985; for research in music perception establishing the salience of contoural turning points; Bolinger 1958, 1986; Cooper et al. 1983; Cruttenden 1986; Thomassen 1982, for corresponding evidence from studies of speech intonation. Studies of visual perception (Attneave 1954; Baker and Loeb 1973) have found analogous inclinations to give more attention to visual "corners," suggesting that the emphatic role of turning points in both vision and audition is generated by a general perceptual strategy, perhaps based upon gestalt law of "common fate" (See Divenyi and Hirsh 1978; Heise and Miller 1951; Watkins and Dyson 1985).

8. This association—as well as other cross-linguistic associations of peaks—does not apply to tonal languages (such as Chinese), where change in the pitch pattern of a word may change its meaning.

9. Recent studies by psychologist Jeanne Bamberger provide an interesting corroboration, within a musical context, of this association. Bamberger reports (personal communication) that subjects with little or no musical training consistently described open musical phrases (such as antecedent phrases in a period) as "ascending," and closed ones (such as consequent phrases) as "descending," regardless of (and often in contradiction to) their actual melodic contour.

10. See also Lakoff and Johnson's (1980) discussion of the "up-down" metaphor.

11. I must stress, however, that nowhere in this book is it claimed that peaks—in music or else-

problem: how are the primitive, "natural" connotations of contour expressed within the stylistic constraints governing a complex, highly developed body of music? As a way of dealing with this problem, I proposed two related hypotheses.

1. Distinctiveness of peaks. *Melodic peaks are associated in a statistically significant way with specific features or configurations in musical dimensions other than contour.*

In other words, if melodic contour is important in a body of music, it will affect other aspects of this music. This effect should be made manifest by examining the phenomena associated with contour's most salient point—the melodic peak. Thus, the hypothesis suggests that the distribution of features in musical domains other than melodic shape (e.g., melodic intervals, durational values, scale degrees) would be different at peaks than at other melodic points: some features would be significantly more frequent at peaks than elsewhere, while others would be less frequent.

If peaks are associated with emphasis and with heightened intensity and tension, they should be coordinate with other emphatic or intensifying features. Thus, I proposed a second, more specific hypothesis.

2. *Melodic peaks are significantly related to emphatic, intensifying, or tension-raising features, elements, or configurations in musical domains other than contour.*[12]

Emphasis, Intensity, and Tension: A Clarification

In this study the notion of *emphasis* is used in a very general sense, denoting "anything that is relatively attention-getting in a time-pattern" (Jones 1987: 622).[13] *Intensity* is used here within a conceptual background such as the intensification-abatement model (Hopkins 1990, chapter 2; Berry 1976), postulating that some musical parameters have two opposing directions of change: one intensifying, namely, promoting activity and elevating tension, the other abating, namely, lessening activity and lowering tension. The related concept of musical *tension* refers here to an unstable, "open," state, strongly implying continuation and resolution.

---

where—function in the same ways universally (actually, the present book shows that they function quite differently even in Western styles based on similar syntactic principles). Rather, the studies referred to here suggest that the perception and use of contour (hence of peaks) is not as strongly bounded by learned, style-specific constraints as that of dimensions such as scales, tonal relationships, or intervals.

12. This hypothesis is supported by recent empirical studies, which indicate that congruence of melodic accents (e.g., melodic turning points, such as peaks, and notes following large pitch intervals) with durational and metric emphasis enhances their perceptual salience. For instance, congruence of durational, metric, and melodic accents improved results in melodic dictation (Boltz and Jones 1986), and in similarity judgment (Monahan, Kendall, and Carterette 1987). It also enhanced detection of melodic changes (Jones, Boltz, and Kidd 1982), and correctness of performance (Drake, Dowling, and Palmer 1991). As Drake and Palmer (1993) show, the perception of melodic accent is strongly affected by interaction with other types of accent.

13. Jones uses "accent" rather than "emphasis." Meyer (1956: 103) suggests a similar definition: "Basically anything is accented when it is marked for consciousness in some way."

The relationship of musical emphasis to events conveying high intensity and tension is complex and often equivocal. On the one hand, structurally significant emphasis is often associated with points of relative stability (such as cadences), or with conclusions of abating processes. On the other, conspicuous emphasis is also related to climactic peaks of intensity and to tension-raising, highly unstable events, such as unprepared dissonances or metric syncopation. A double edged notion of emphasis, inspired by an eighteenth- and nineteenth-century music-theoretical tradition, may clarify this dichotomy. I present this notion not as an all-inclusive, either-or theoretical distinction. It is suggested as a clarification of an incongruity embodied in notions of salience in music, an incongruity that may manifest itself in a study of an emphatic musical phenomenon such as the melodic peak.

Emphatic events seem to fall into two distinct categories we may term "grammatical" and "rhetorical." [14] Events that are *grammatically* emphasized are points of stability in the musical flow, serving to elucidate musical structure. Such events are marked because they are higher than others in a specific musical hierarchy: for instance, a metric downbeat relative to the surrounding up- and offbeats, structural melodic notes relative to those embellishing them, or (in a piece employing traditional contrapuntal principles) harmonic consonances relative to the dissonances they resolve. *Rhetorically* emphasized events, on the other hand, capture our attention because they are particularly striking, exceptional, or surprising. They are emphatic because of their potential for arousal; thus, they need not be tonally, metrically, or otherwise stable. Rhetorical emphasis can be the result of sudden changes, exceptional features, or high intensity in various domains: for instance, a dynamic *sforzando*, wide melodic leaps, or striking dissonances. Often the very feature that generates rhetorical emphasis (for instance, sharp harmonic dissonance) would hinder grammatical emphasis.

In tonal music, a paradigm for grammatical emphasis is a conclusive authentic cadence, where stable, hierarchically superior configurations in the harmonic, melodic and rhythmic domains coincide. The paradigm for rhetorical emphasis is perhaps a climax or "structural highpoint" (Agawu 1982), where several parameters

---

14. My notion of "grammatical" versus "rhetorical" emphasis is similar to and extends concepts found in eighteenth- and nineteenth-century theories of musical performance. Mattheson's "accent" and "emphasis" are an early example of a similar distinction between aspects of musical emphasis. Later in the eighteenth century, several writers presented similar classifications of emphasis, such as that between "grammatical," "oratorical," and "pathetic" accents, found (among other places) in Rousseau (1768/1969): 2ff and in Koch (1802): 50–53 (see also Ratner 1982, chapter 11). In the nineteenth century, Lussy's distinction of metric, rhythmic, and "pathetic" accents (Lussy 1874) continues this tradition.

Though such performance-oriented notions are not as common in recent theoretical writings, a distinction between hierarchical superiority and "phenomenal" emphasis is acknowledged by many (see, e.g., Agawu 1982). Especially well known is the discussion of "kinds of accent" in Lerdahl and Jackendoff (1983): 17–18. Lerdahl and Jackendoff's approach, however, suggests (unlike my rather "oppositional" classification) a hierarchy of types of emphasis, where phenomenal accents constitute meter, and both phenomenal and metric accents take part in establishing structural accent.

are at the zenith of their intensity curves. Hence, one may expect to find phenomena related to rhetorical (rather than grammatical) emphasis at melodic peaks.

CONTOUR AND OTHER MUSICAL DIMENSIONS: SECONDARY HYPOTHESES

To test my hypotheses statistically, I formulated a number of more specific hypotheses about particular emphatic, tensional, or intensifying features, and about their association with melodic peaks. In choosing the features to be examined, I used two general criteria. First, I selected features widely considered intensifying, tensional, or emphatic (in the senses specified here) by musicians, music theorists, or psychologists. When possible, I chose features whose roles in music perception have been empirically examined. Second, to minimize the possibility that my initial hypotheses would grossly determine the raw data, I chose features whose presence in a particular musical sample could be rigorously and mechanically determined. This limitation inevitably leads to significant tradeoffs. In particular, it precludes (or at least immensely complicates) the analysis of higher-level pitch and durational relationships.[15] Such obviously important aspects of musical structure, though not examined in the "hard," statistical parts of this study, were considered in a complementary "soft" analysis (e.g., chapter 5, "melodic patterns").

Duration, Rhythm, and Meter

I hypothesized that peaks concur with both durational (agogic) emphasis and metric accent, and alternatively with syncopation. I also suggested that peaks are often the first or last notes in a musical segment, and frequently occur at later parts of pieces or segments.

---

15. At least two considerations complicate a quantitative or statistical analysis of such above-surface relationships. First, to determine in a rigorous, formal way an intervallic or durational relation between nonadjacent notes (or units), one needs a consistent method for selecting these notes. Such a method would most likely need to balance different selection rules against one another, and (if selection were to be computable) quantify the strengths of various selection rules (an intuitive, noncomputable method is, of course, possible and perhaps desirable, but might lead to reliance on one's initial hypothesis). Such a quantification is not only beyond the scope of this work; it also requires "a much better understanding of many difficult musical and psychological issues than exists at present" (Lerdahl and Jackendoff 1983: 55), particularly when selection criteria based on local features are to be balanced against those based on global characteristics. Second, the related problem of level-equivalency further complicates statistical analysis of such relationships. A statistical examination of intervallic, durational, or tonal relationships above the musical "surface" necessitates some measure of equivalency of hierarchic levels which could be applied to different pieces (and in our case, to pieces of extremely different styles, genres, formal structures, and durations). The problem of finding such a measure is, again, beyond the scope of this work.

Durational emphasis. A note longer than those surrounding it is durationally emphasized. The notion of durational emphasis is one of the most well-established in rhythmic theory. It is supported by a long music-theoretical tradition (e.g., Koch 1802, Lussy 1874, and particularly Riemann 1884) as well as recent theories of rhythmic articulation (Cooper and Meyer 1960; Narmour 1977, 1990). The psychological reality of durational emphasis has been repeatedly corroborated by studies of music perception (e.g., Jones 1987; Drake, Dowling, and Palmer 1991; Drake and Palmer 1993) and speech intonation (Carlson et al. 1975; see also Cruttenden 1986: 16).[16]

I suggest, then, that melodic peaks, as emphatic phenomena, are characteristically longer than the notes surrounding them.

Metric emphasis. Metric structure orders a temporal flow into a hierarchy of regularly occurring accents, points of metric emphasis. [17] The accents are generated and supported by various cues at the musical surface, including salient phenomena in various musical dimensions (see, e.g., Lerdahl and Jackendoff 1983, Chapter 4).[18] Because melodic peaks are important agents of emphasis, they would function as cues. Hence, I hypothesized that peaks often coincide with points of metric accentuation.[19]

Syncopation. Syncopation, which involves a conflict between a metric structure and the rhythmic surface, has traditionally been regarded an emphasizing strategy. In the terms presented above, syncopation is an example of rhetorical emphasis, generating surprise and tension. Hence, as a possible alternative to the metric emphasis hypothesis, I suggested that a peak is often a syncopating note.[20]

Temporal location. The location of peaks in segments of various sizes and in entire pieces is relevant to issues of emphasis and tension in several ways. First, discussions of the "dynamic curve" often suggest that the climax of this prototypical process, its "structural highpoint," is typically located late in a piece or segment (Agawu 1982, chapter 1; Toch 1948: 81–86). If melodic peaks are indeed frequently associated with points of heightened intensity, they would also be associated with

---

16. Perceptually, durational emphasis may be accounted for by a combination of two tendencies: the inclination to perceive rhythmic closure when a short note moves to a longer one (cf. Cooper and Meyer 1960, Lerdahl and Jackendoff 1983, Narmour 1990, for music-theoretical accounts; Deliege 1987, Garner and Gottwald 1986, Woodrow 1951, for empirical corroboration), and the tendency to perceive the last event of a group as accented (Jones 1987, Wright et al. 1985).

17. For definitions and discussions of metric structure in music-theoretical studies see Benjamin 1984, Berry 1976, 1985, Cooper and Meyer 1960, Hasty 1997, Lerdahl and Jackendoff 1983, Narmour 1990. For an extensive bibliography see Kramer 1985. A survey of recent empirical studies concerning the perception of metric structure appears in Narmour 1990, chapter 11.

18. Once established, however, metric structure tends to persist for some time even in the absence of any supporting surface phenomena. See Thomassen 1982.

19. Thomassen's model of melodic accent (1982), recently corroborated by a statistical study of diverse musical repertories (Huron and Royal 1996), supports this hypothesis by assigning stronger stress to contoural "corners," particularly those terminating an ascent.

20. The hypotheses concerning metric emphasis and syncopation are inconsistent with regard to each case, but in an entire "population" both can prove to be significantly associated with peaks.

such climactic loci. Thus, one may expect peaks to appear more frequently in the later parts of a segment or a composition.[21]

Second, studies of short-term memory indicate that the first and last events or items in a series are recalled more readily than others (Wright et al. 1985; also see Jones 1987). This suggests that the first and last notes in a segment would be emphasized. Accordingly, peaks (as points of emphasis) would frequently be the initial or terminal notes in a segment.

Melodic Aspects

Several secondary hypotheses concern aspects of melodic configuration. I suggested that peaks are approached by relatively large pitch intervals, often appear only once in a segment, and are associated with successive pitch repetitions.[22]

Melodic emphasis. A relatively large leap that separates a note from preceding pitches significantly emphasizes that note. The larger the leap preceding a note, the stronger the melodic emphasis that note receives. The perceptual reality of this phenomenon has been repeatedly corroborated by studies of melodic perception (Jones 1987, Monahan, Kendall, and Carterette 1987) and of musical performance (Drake and Palmer 1993, Sundberg et al. 1991).[23] An analogous tendency was found in speech intonation.[24]

Melodic emphasis is strongly related to heightened tension. Musicians from Zarlino to Jeppesen have noted the arousing effect of large skips, suggesting this unsettling effect as a reason for the prevalence of stepwise progressions in music.[25] While such remarks are mostly confined to specific Western styles, experimental studies of emotional expression in speech intonation (Fonagy and Magdics 1972; Williams and Stevens 1972) and cross-cultural kinesthetic studies (Clynes and Nettheim

21. Huron's statistical analysis of register in Western folksongs (1996) corroborates this hypothesis for both single phrases and entire songs.

22. Tonal facets of melody are addressed separately.

23. Two principal explanations were given to the perceived salience of large melodic leaps. Jones 1987 and others suggest that the emphatic effect of large leaps stems from their rarity in most musical repertories. (See Deutsch 1978; Dowling and Harwood 1985; Ortmann 1926, 1937; Vos and Troost 1989; Watt 1923. Also relevant are Carlsen's studies of melodic expectancy, 1981.) A relatively large leap would create "a local surprise of 'differentness'" (Jones 1987) and would be thus marked for attention. Another explanation relates melodic emphasis to the Gestalt law of proximity, suggesting that melodic distance emphasizes a note because it detaches it from the preceding sequence. See Bregman's experiments concerning "streaming," in Bregman 1990; Bregman and Campbell 1971; and Lerdahl and Jackendoff's "Grouping Preference Rules" (1983: 43–52).

24. Greater pitch change marks emphasis in speech: the emphasized words in a sentence include quicker and larger fundamental frequency changes, while syllables neighboring them include lesser fundamental frequency movements (Carlson et al. 1975, 1989).

25. "Wide distances . . . produce a kind of distress in the ear. Let us than avoid these distances to make our counterpoint pleasing" (Zarlino 1558/1986 [pt. 3]: 78).

1982) suggest that the association of large pitch intervals with tension and forceful affect is a very general phenomenon. In examining melodic emphasis at peaks, then, I investigated the interaction of two prominent, perhaps universal, factors in melodic emphasis and expression: contour and interval size.[26]

I hypothesized that melodic peaks are normally approached (and possibly also left)[27] by relatively large pitch intervals.[28]

Pitch-register singularity. I assumed that a pitch that appears only once within a segment is emphasized. Presumably, the "freshness" and uniqueness of such a pitch marks it for attention. Musicians have suggested that such emphasis-by-uniqueness is particularly appropriate for melodic peaks, because recurrence of a peak note wears out its climactic effect, and obscures melodic shape.[29] However, no studies known to me have empirically tested whether this procedure has been heeded by composers. This study proposes such a test, hypothesizing that peaks characteristically appear only once in the segment they climax.

Repeated pitches. Some musicians have suggested that the emphatic effect of a high note is enhanced when it is repeated in succession (see, for instance, Mattheson 1981: 370). Accordingly, I proposed that peaks often appear as a succession of repeated pitches.

26. Of course, size is not the only factor determining the degree of tension conveyed by a melodic interval: a leap of a seventh, for instance, would convey a much stronger tension than the larger leap of an octave. Several additional factors may affect the perception of tension conveyed by a melodic interval. For one, measures of pitch distance other than that of interval size contribute to the perception of intervallic tension: notes in the same position on the pitch "chroma" (e.g., notes an octave apart; see Shepard's 1982 "tonal helix" model) or close to each other on the circle of 5ths may be perceived as similar, though they are, measured in interval size, wide apart. The tonal context further influences the perception of "distance" between successive notes (see Krumhansl 1990 for recent studies of this issue), and thus, presumably, the degree of tension and emphasis conveyed by a change of pitch. In addition, large melodic intervals may be perceived, due to the well-known phenomenon of stream segregation (Bregman and Campbell 1971), as implied harmonic intervals. Thus, their degree of dissonance may add to (as with sevenths) or detract from (as with octaves) the tension they convey.

However, both methodological considerations and the empirical results noted above justify, to my mind, a separate consideration of this factor. Together with pitch direction, pitch distance may perhaps be regarded as a primeval, natural factor, interacting with a culture-based tonal language to create the subtle shadings of musical expression.

27. When a peak is both approached and left by large intervals, the ensuing registral isolation may mark it for attention. Hence, one may hypothesize that peaks would be surrounded (rather than just approached) by large intervals. However, this is an equivocal situation: a descending skip from a peak emphasizes it, but given that large intervals stress the note they approach, this skip also emphasizes the note following the peak.

28. This hypothesis is supported by Huron and Royal's finding (1996: 150) that most intervals larger than a tritone are followed by a change of registral direction. Carlsen's study of melodic expectancy (1981) presents similar results. Narmour's notion of "reversal" (1990) suggests a theoretical basis (somewhat different than the one suggested here) for these findings.

29. See, for instance, Toch (1948: 81). "About the climax of a melody we may say, in general: The climax appears only once . . . We are sensitive to [the peaks'] repeated exposure . . . An overdose of such exposure has a blurring effect on the line's contour." Also see Jeppesen (1939: 95).

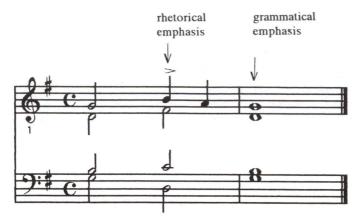

EXAMPLE 1.2A. "Grammatical" and "rhetorical" harmonic emphases.

EXAMPLE 1.2B. A linear analysis of Example 1.2a.

Harmonic and Tonal Features

In the tonal repertories considered in this study, I have related the first principal hypothesis, postulating distinctiveness of peaks, to *chord structure*, the morphology of the chord associated with a peak (e.g., a major triad, a diminished-seventh chord); to the identity of this chord as a *harmonic scale degree* (I, ii, etc.) in the prevailing tonality; and to the "*soprano position*" of the peak, namely its role (e.g., root, third, etc.) in this chord. I also considered the *melodic scale degree* ($\hat{1}$, $\hat{2}$, etc.) of the peak itself. Thus, I suggested that peaks are associated with specific chord morphologies, harmonic and melodic scale-degrees, and soprano positions.

It is more difficult to relate the second principal hypothesis (suggesting an association of peaks with emphatic, tensional or intensifying features) to harmonic dimensions, because it is in the domain of harmony that the dichotomy between "grammatical" and "rhetorical" emphasis most clearly manifests itself. For instance, which of the four events in Example 1.2a is emphasized? Linear analysis (Example 1.2b) shows that the upper line prolongs the tonic note G by way of its upper neighbor, A, while the later is itself ornamented by the appoggiatura note B. Hence, the first and particularly the last event in the phrase, its most stable, "structural" note and chord, are *grammatically* emphasized. The least stable event in the phrase, and thus the least emphasized grammatically, is the V^{13}_7 chord underlying the peak, the appoggiatura note B. From the standpoint of tonal syntax, this note is merely an embellishment of an embellishment: a transient dissonance elaborating an event that is itself subsidiary to the concluding tonic.[30]

Rhetorically, however, this appoggiatura is the most intense and emphatic event in the phrase. Moreover, the same factors that de-emphasize the appoggiatura grammatically—unstable dominant harmony and a sharp dissonance—emphasize it rhetorically. Especially, the striking, unprepared dissonance created by the non-harmonic tone B makes this event conspicuous and implies emphasis in performance.[31]

Are peaks associated with features (such as striking dissonances) that generate tension and high intensity (and hence "rhetorical" emphasis)? Or are they associated with features strengthening tonal stability (and thus enhancing "grammatical" emphasis), such as consonant chords and stable scale degrees? The answers to these questions form part of the results of this study.

Dynamic Emphasis

A large body of evidence—including empirical research on music perception and performance (Nakamura 1987; Williams 1990; Drake and Palmer 1993; Friberg 1991) advice in performance manuals (e.g., Türk 1789), statistical studies of some musical repertories (Sheer 1989), studies of speech intonation (Hart et al. 1990), and (to some extent) psychoacoustical investigation (Fletcher 1953: 188)[32]—indicate that as-

30. Some Schenkerian analysts may interpret the highpoint of this phrase as a structural $\hat{3}$, transferred from an inner voice in the opening tonic chord (and thus as a "grammatically emphasized" note). Though some contexts may support this interpretation, it is baseless in this context-free example.

31. Dissonances, in particular those deviating from the normative tertial sonority, such as appoggiaturas, have traditionally been related to powerful affect, heightened tension, and strong emphasis. Eighteenth- and nineteenth-century performance manuals often recommend the performer to emphasize such dissonances forcefully. For instance, Türk (1789: chapter 6), who categorizes dissonant chords according to their "harshness" and relates the degree of harshness to the degree of emphasis demanded in performance, includes such dissonances—for instance 9th chords or a cadential "VII" suspended over a tonic bass note—in the group of chords demanding the strongest emphasis. Well known also is the customary emphasis given to appoggiaturas over the chords they "lean" upon (see, e.g., Bach 1949: 322). The association of appoggiaturas with striking emotional effect, and hence with marked "rhetorical" salience, is also supported by studies of affective response to music (Sloboda 1992).

32. The well-known "Fletcher-Munson" curves indicate that different degrees of intensities (in decibels) are needed in different frequencies in order to produce an equal degree of perceived loudness (as measured in phones). Up to a frequency of approximately 4000 cps (around the top range of a piano keyboard), the intensity required to produce a given perceived loudness decreases as the pitch frequency increases. In other words: a given amount of intensity would produce an increasingly louder sound as pitch frequency increases. This psychoacoustic finding may partially explain the "naturalness" of the congruence between a pitch ascent and a crescendo: by correlating pitch ascents with crescendi composers may simply magnify a natural tendency. However, one notes the Fletcher-Munson curves apply

cent in pitch tends to correlate with increase in dynamics. Accordingly, I hypothesized that pitch peaks are frequently associated with dynamic peaks, such as culminations of crescendi or strong dynamic accents, thus receiving a "dynamic emphasis." [33]

THE REPERTORIES

The core of this book consists of three separate studies of melodic peaks, each testing my hypotheses in a specific musical corpus. The first study concerns an early Classic repertory (Haydn's early keyboard sonatas and dramatic works); the second deals with a well-known Romantic repertory (Chopin's waltzes and mazurkas); the third investigates a body of twentieth-century music (Alban Berg's post-tonal compositions).[34] None of these disparate repertories necessarily represents its epoch or style period: I chose them simply because I was interested in studying contour in diverse musical contexts. A statistical study of peaks that traced a diachronic process in music from a wide chronological section (in a manner analogous to that of Gjerdingen's study of melodic schemata, 1988) would certainly be a worthwhile endeavor. Here, however, I chose to illuminate in some depth specific bodies of music, rather than glance, through representative samples, at broad style-periods.

Nevertheless, I also chose to dedicate an entire chapter (Chapter 6) to a statistical comparison of these three repertories. The choice of such diverse repertories for a comparative study may seem questionable. One might question not only the significance of comparing bodies of music that are not necessarily representative of larger stylistic corpora, but particularly the comparison of tonal repertories with a post-tonal one, whose pitch structure is based upon entirely different principles.

The very diversity of the examined music, however, makes a comparison worthwhile. For instance, though it would not indicate that they are applicable to all Western music, confirmation of my hypotheses in these three repertories would show that their applicability transcends the confines of any particular stylistic domain. It would thus support the view that the "natural" psychological basis of contour can surpass the limits of a specific period style or the constraints of a particular pitch grammar.

clearly to sinusoidal tones only, and their relevance to the more complex tones used in music is therefore questionable.

33. This study also investigates some inter-parametric relationships. Because of the technical nature of this facet of the study, I presented it (with the appropriate secondary hypotheses) in the next chapter.

34. In each of these repertories pieces of different genres or performance media were examined. I compared the different genres or performance media included in each sample (i.e., waltzes versus mazurkas in Chopin, or instrumental versus vocal music in Haydn and Berg). I discovered few statistically significant differences in these comparisons (see Eitan 1991, vol. 2, app. 4–8). With regard to the questions considered in this study, the roles of genre and performance medium seem to be small within the styles examined. Hence, the fact that these variables differ also between styles (for instance, that the Haydn sample includes vocal music, while the Chopin sample does not) does not pose a serious methodological problem in comparing these styles.

Conversely, refutation of my hypotheses in these three repertories would undermine the view that the use of melodic contour in Western music is based upon universal psychological constraints.

The repertory chosen enables us to compare the treatment of peaks in styles where intervallic pitch structure is ruled by entirely different systems, namely, Berg's post-tonal music on the one hand, Chopin's and Haydn's, both operating within "common practice" tonal language, on the other. One may ask whether the two styles that share a system of functional pitch hierarchy would also be similar with respect to melodic contour. Correspondingly, one may question whether the vast difference in pitch "grammar" that separates the Berg repertory from the tonal-functional music investigated here is paralleled by a considerable difference concerning contour.

Such comparison may shed some light on the status of melodic contour vis-à-vis the tonal-functional or intervallic syntax of pitch. Accepted notions of musical structure often relegate "gestural" aspects of music, such as melodic contour (or, for that matter, dynamics, attack rate, or textural density), to a marginal role. These are regarded as secondary parameters, serving mainly to highlight events in supposedly more substantial domains, such as form or the tonal structure of pitch. Insofar as the perception of melody is concerned, recent psychological studies draw, as we have seen, a very different picture: they view tonal relationships and melodic contour as two distinct domains of melodic perception, the latter often predominating in delineating perceived melodic structure.

If contour is subsidiary to the tonal-functional or intervallic syntax of pitch, one may expect that styles sharing a common pitch syntax (in our case, Haydn's and Chopin's) would be closer with regard to the treatment of contour than styles whose pitch-structure is based on different principles (e.g., Chopin and Berg). If, on the other hand, contour is an independent dimension of melodic style (as studies of melodic perception would imply), affinity of tonal syntax need not correlate with similarity of contour configuration: repertories sharing a tonal syntax may considerably differ in their treatment of contour, while ones whose pitch structures are based on different systems may handle contour similarly.

The selected repertory also makes it possible to examine bodies of music whose modes of expression are commonly contrasted as "classic" versus "romantic," namely, Haydn on the one hand, Chopin—and in a sense also Berg—on the other. There is one reason this rather simplistic stylistic dichotomy may be of interest in the context of this study. This is the high regard given by the ideology of nineteenth-century Romanticism to the use of "natural" means of expression, and its disdain of previous (namely, eighteenth-century) reliance on learned, conventional expressive gestures. A study dealing with the roles of a dimension such as contour, with its "natural" connotations, may indicate whether and how such ideological concerns are expressed in the configuration of melodic style.[35]

---

35. This point is elaborated in chapters 4–6. Also see Meyer 1989, chapters 6 and 7.

OVERVIEW

This study examines features and structures affiliated with melodic peaks in three musical repertories, and interprets the results of this inquiry in light of the aforementioned hypotheses. My research methods are described in Chapter 2, which presents the statistical procedure used to test the hypotheses (basically, comparing the frequencies of selected features in a group of peaks with their frequencies in a group of "control" notes), describes how peaks and controls were selected, and defines the features whose relationships to peaks were investigated. Chapters 3–5 present and discuss the statistical analysis of the Haydn, Chopin, and Berg samples. In each of these three chapters, "hard" statistical analyses are followed by "softer" interpretations of the results. By determining which features are significantly associated with peaks, statistical analysis tests the primary and secondary hypotheses presented above. I then interpret the statistical results, relate them to the hypotheses, and, using musical analyses of selected examples, discuss gestures characteristically associated with peaks in each repertory. Each chapter closes with a section that assesses the structural and expressive roles of melodic peaks in the style discussed, and relates findings concerning contour to other characteristics of the style.

Chapter 6 presents the results of a statistical analysis comparing peaks in the three bodies of music. This comparison acts as the point of departure for a discussion of two general issues: the treatment of contour peaks as reflecting cultural stances toward "natural" psychological aptitudes, and the relationships of gestural aspects of a style, such as melodic contour, to its syntactical aspects, such as functional pitch structure.

CHAPTER 2

Method: Testing the Hypotheses

SELECTION OF PEAKS AND CONTROL NOTES

In each of the three examined repertories I compared a group of melodic peaks with a control group of randomly selected notes. To make the analysis methodologically sound, I defined precise procedures for selecting peaks and controls.

Selection of peaks. After segmenting each composition into its principal sections, I selected in each section the highest pitch of the main melodic part (usually the upper line).[1] In Chopin's Mazurka in F♯ minor, Opus 6 No. 1, for instance, I selected the opening notes of measures 13 (E^5) and 17 ($C\sharp^6$), one being the highest pitch (in its first appearance) of the opening period (measures 1–16), the other, the highest pitch in the next section (measures 17–40).

Whenever a piece follows a conventional formal scheme, I read the scheme as the basis for segmentation (this was the case, for instance, in Haydn's minuets). Similarly, when the principal sections of a piece are unequivocally indicated (for instance, in Berg's *Lulu*, which is mostly segmented into clear operatic "numbers"), I followed such indications. If there is a text, I also considered its segmentation.[2] Where neither conventional form nor the composer's indications provide a clear basis for segmentation, I used cadential articulation (in the two tonal samples) and Gestalt-like grouping criteria such as temporal and registral proximity, parametric similarity, symmetry, and parallelism of segments as the basis for segmentation.[3]

---

1. If a peak is repeated within the section, I examined its first appearance. An examination of all the appearances of a peak pitch would have given undue weight in the statistical analysis to pieces whose peak pitch is repeated several times. For the sake of consistency, I selected the first appearance of the peak for examination in all pieces. This decision does not imply that first appearances of peaks are generally more (or less) important or climactic than later ones.

2. The examination of some characteristics involved segmentation into several levels. See the "temporal location" and "pitch-register singularity" characteristics described below.

3. These criteria are derived from general perceptual principles suggested by psychologists of the

EXAMPLE 2.1. Chopin, Waltz in E♭ Major, Opus 18, measures 1–12.

The designation of a peak as simply the highest pitch in a given segment should be emphasized. One might object to such a "mechanical" stipulation, claiming that in many cases the highest pitch serves a merely ornamental function, and the "real," structural peak is a different note. For example, one could argue that in the opening phrase of Example 2.1 the "real" peak is not the highest pitch (C^6, measure 9) but the more structural $B♭^5$ that precedes it (measure 8). The point of this study, however, is to isolate one aspect of musical organization—contour—and then examine its interactions with other parameters. In this way we can investigate (at least in part) whether, how, and to what extent a contoural phenomenon—the peak, as defined here—becomes a point of structural and expressive importance. To investigate only the "structural" peaks would beg the question. Therefore, I considered the highest pitch in a section a peak—even if it is clearly an embellishment. Indeed, one of the intriguing questions about peaks is what functions they perform when they are not "structural highpoints."

Selection of controls. The control group consists of notes from the repertory investigated, randomly chosen with the aid of computer-generated sequences of random numbers.[4] These numbers were assigned, in a predetermined order, to the pieces from which melodic peaks were selected. For instance, I assigned the first 50 numbers in the Chopin sequence to waltzes, in opus-number order, and the following 50 numbers

Gestalt tradition such as Köhler, Koffka, and Wertheimer in the 1920s and '30s. Meyer, Narmour, and Lerdahl and Jackendoff are among recent music theorists who have explicitly used Gestalt principles in musical analysis. For a recent formal representation of such criteria, see the "Grouping Preference Rules" (GFR) 1–6 in Lerdahl and Jackendoff (1983): 43–52.

4. Sequences of random numbers were generated by an IBM-PC, using LOTUS 1-2-3 Random Number Generator (see Appendix 2).

to mazurkas (again, in opus-number order). To determine the control notes, I used the random numbers as order numbers of notes in the upper lines of these pieces. For example, if number 105 was assigned to a piece, the 105th note in the upper line of this piece was the control note.

Sample size. The Haydn sample includes 119 peaks and 119 controls (68 notes from keyboard sonatas, 51 from operas). The Chopin sample includes 97 peaks (46 from waltzes, 51 from mazurkas) and 100 controls (50 from waltzes, 50 from mazurkas). The Berg sample includes 86 peaks and 86 controls (35 from instrumental pieces, 51 from vocal ones).[5] For some features actual samples were somewhat smaller than the numbers given above, because not all features were applicable for all notes (for instance, last notes in pieces or movements do not have an interval following them). Altogether, I examined 302 peaks and 305 controls in the three repertoires.

THE STATISTICAL PROCEDURE

Characteristics or relationships (described below) of each of the selected notes—peaks and controls—were examined.[6] For each of the three repertoires, I compared the frequency of these characteristics in the peaks and controls. To determine whether differences between peaks and controls are statistically significant, I used two statistical tests. The first and principal test was a chi-square test of homogeneity. This test is designed to determine if two "populations" (here, the melodic peaks in an examined repertory and the entire "population" of notes that compose the principal melodic lines in this repertory) differ from each other with respect to the data distribution concerning a given variable (e.g., the distribution of the different intervals in the two groups). As a complementary and more specific procedure I used a standard score (z) test to compare the proportions of a particular characteristic or relationship in the two groups. Thus, I used a chi-square test to determine whether in the Chopin sample the peaks differ from the controls (representing the entire population of melodic notes) with respect to the distribution of intervals as a whole, while I used a standard score test to determine whether the proportions of a specific interval (e.g., perfect fifth) are significantly different in the two groups.[7]

In addition to a statistical analysis of each sample separately, I compared results among the three repertoires. I was not interested in differences in the distributions of the examined features per se (e.g., differences between the Chopin and Berg repertories as to the distribution of intervals). Rather, I investigated whether, with regard

5. A sample size of at least thirty specimens is normally considered appropriate for statistical analysis of the kind employed here.

6. A tabulation of all the data collected in the three repertoires is featured in Eitan (1991), vol. 2, app. 1–3.

7. In examining durational, metric, and melodic emphasis (see below) I used (in addition to comparisons of peaks and controls) a computation testing the null hypothesis (H0) that the proportions (P) of emphasized and deemphasized peaks are equal (H0: P(plus) = P(minus)).

to each feature, the relation between peaks and controls is different in different repertories (for instance, whether the Chopin and Berg repertories exhibit comparable differences between peaks and controls concerning the distribution of intervals). To examine such issues, I used a three-dimensional chi-square test, which determined whether the ratios between peaks and controls are, for each feature, significantly different in the Haydn, Chopin, and Berg repertories.

CHARACTERISTICS AND RELATIONSHIPS EXAMINED

To address the secondary hypotheses proposed in chapter 1, I defined procedures for examining a number of specific musical features. I describe each of these features below and explain how I tested them.

Durational and Metric Relationships

Durational emphasis. To test the hypothesis that peaks tend to be emphasized durationally, I separately compared the duration of each selected note with the duration of each of its two neighbors, and designated the longer of each pair of consecutive notes as *durationally emphasized.*[8] For instance, in Example 2.2 the peak (F♯[6], measure 13), an eighth note, is durationally less emphasized than its immediate predecessor (a dotted quarter), but receives (at least as notated) the same durational emphasis as the following note, also an eighth note.

I tested the hypothesis that peaks would be associated with metrical accentuation by examining each note in two related, complementary ways: in terms of its place in the metric hierarchy, as determined by its location within the measure ("metric location"), and in terms of the note's metric emphasis in relation to its two immediate neighbors ("metric emphasis"). In addition, I examined whether a selected note is syncopating.

Metric location. I determined the metric location of each note's attack, using categories such as: on 1st beat; on 2nd beat; off 1st beat; off 2nd beat, etc. To compare results in pieces differing metrically, I also used broader categories: on 1st beat; on another beat; on an off-beat.

Metric emphasis. Given two consecutive notes, the note higher up in the metric hierarchy (e.g., a note whose attack falls on the first beat in the measure versus one whose attack falls on another beat; or any on-beat versus any off-beat attack) is the metrically emphasized of the two. I determined whether each of the selected notes is more, less or equally emphasized metrically than each of its two immediate neigh-

---

8. When a rest follows an examined note, I added the duration of this rest to the duration of the note preceding it. Thus, duration was measured (in the relevant melodic part) from one attack to the next.

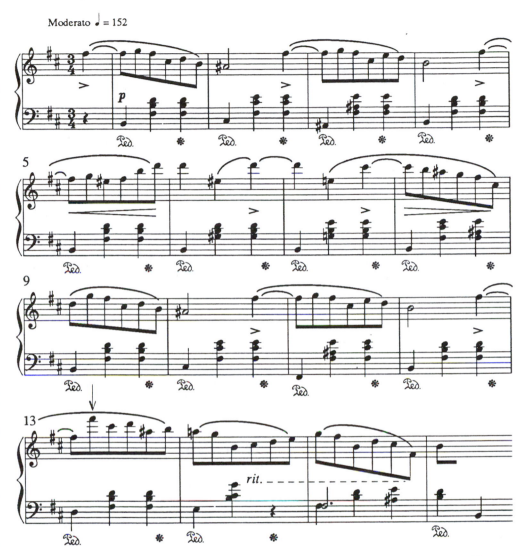

EXAMPLE 2.2. Chopin, Waltz in B Minor, Opus 69 No. 2 (Fontana Version), measures 1–16.

bors. Thus the peak note C^6 in Example 2.1 is metrically less emphasized than the preceding down-beat Bb^5, but more emphasized than the succeeding off-beat Bb^5.

Syncopation. I investigated whether syncopation is significantly associated with peaks by comparing the frequency of syncopating notes in the peaks and control groups.

I considered as syncopations rhythms such as that in Example 2.3a, where a rest occurs on an accent or beat, and stress is thus shifted to the preceding note; and rhythms such as that in Example 2.3b, where a note attacked on a relatively unac-

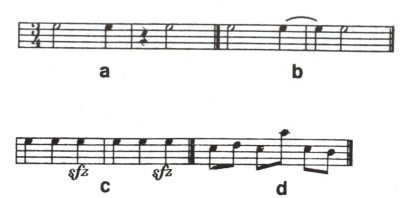

EXAMPLE 2.3. Syncopation.

cented metric locus is tied to an accented one. Rhythms such as that in Example 2.3c, where a normally unaccented beat is dynamically stressed, and 2.3d, where the "phenomenal accent" generated by the peak itself emphasizes a metrically unaccented note, are considered elsewhere: the former under "dynamic emphasis," the latter under "metric location."

 Temporal location. To test the hypotheses that peaks are frequently featured late in segments, and often appear as first or last notes, I determined the location of each of the examined notes at three levels of segmentation. The lowest level was a period, a phrase group, or another segment comparable in length (roughly 8–16 measures). The next unit in the segmentation hierarchy (e.g., a double period) constitute the middle level. Finally, I determined the location of selected notes within a larger, higher level section, such as a sonata-form exposition or the first part of a binary aria.[9] Each level of segmentation was divided into four equal, arbitrary units, and I noted in which of these four quarters the examined note occurred. For instance, in Example 2.2 the peak—F♯[6], measure 13—is located in the last quarter of the extracted segment, measures 1–16. For each level of segmentation, the distributions of peaks and controls in the four quarters were noted, as were cases in which the examined note is the first or last note within a segment.

Melodic Relationships: Intervals, Tonal Function, and Melodic Gestures

I related melodic contour to several other aspects of melody. To test the secondary hypothesis that melodic emphasis is a characteristic of peaks, I examined the immediate melodic-intervallic relations of each selected note in two ways (see "intervals" and "melodic emphasis" below). I determined each note's tonal status, that is, its scale-degree identity. In addition, I examined whether selected notes are unique within segments, and whether they are associated with successions of repeated notes.

 9. In short pieces, such as Haydn's minuets, I considered only two levels of segmentation.

EXAMPLE 2.4. Chopin, Mazurka in A Minor, Opus 7 No. 2, measures 41–48.

Interval identity. I determined the identity of the melodic intervals by which each peak or control note is approached and left.[10]

Ascending and descending intervals. Large ascending intervals are generally more frequent than large descending intervals (Vos and Troost 1989). Because approaches to peaks are necessarily ascending, and the intervals following them necessarily descending, it could be that any finding regarding the intervals surrounding peaks merely reflects this general tendency, rather than a tendency specifically associated with peaks. To address this issue, I examined whether interval distribution in ascents toward peaks is significantly different from the distribution of *ascending* intervals in the controls. Similarly, I compared the interval distribution in descents from peaks with that of *descending* intervals in the controls.

Melodic emphasis. Given two consecutive notes, the one approached by a larger interval was designated as melodically emphasized (see chapter 1). For instance, in Example 2.8 (p. 30) the peak (Bb^5, measure 14), approached by a minor tenth, receives a stronger melodic emphasis than both its neighbors, approached by smaller intervals: G^4, approached by a minor third, and A^5, approached by a minor second. Each of the selected notes (peak or control) was thus compared to its two neighbors.

Scale degree. In the two tonal repertoires (Haydn and Chopin) I determined the scale-degree identity of the selected notes. Scale degree was examined in terms both of the immediate tonal context, and of the principal tonality of the piece. So, for example, the peak note ($F\sharp^6$, measure 44) in Example 2.4 functions locally as the tonic

10. Note that by definition a peak cannot be approached or left by a prime. For the sake of consistency, primes were also ignored in the control group.

note ($\hat{1}$) in a tonicized F♯ minor area; on a higher level, and with regard to the principal tonic of this mazurka, it functions as the submediant ($\hat{6}$).

The analysis of this dimension also includes a categorization of the selected notes into three hierarchically-ordered groups: the tonic note; the other stable scale-degrees, the tonic triad members $\hat{3}$ and $\hat{5}$; and the unstable degrees $\hat{2}$, $\hat{4}$, $\hat{6}$, and $\hat{7}$.[11]

Repeated pitches. To determine whether this supposed emphatic strategy is indeed utilized in peaks, I compared the frequency of repeated pitch configurations in the peaks and control groups.

Pitch-register singularity. Assuming that a pitch is emphasized if it appears only once within a segment, I examined whether a selected note recurs within its low-level segment or within the entire piece.[12] Whenever a pitch does recur, I also noted whether it recurs as a part of a return of the entire phrase in which it originally appeared, or within a different context.

Harmony: Chord Function and Morphology

To test the secondary hypotheses that peaks are associated with particular harmonic features, I examined the tonal function and the morphology of the chords in which the peaks and controls occur. Thus, I determined for each examined note the harmonic scale degree that underlies it, the structure of the chord of which it is a part, and its soprano position (its relation to the chord's root).[13]

Harmonic degrees. The harmonic scale degree of the chord that contains an examined note was determined in relation to the local (phrase-level) tonality. For instance, the chord that includes the peak note G^5 in measure 18 of Chopin's Opus 24 No. 1 (Example 4.6) is considered a Dominant (V) of the locally tonicized B♭ and is not directly related to the main tonality, G minor.

Chord structure. The classification of chord structure used in this study is not proposed as a generally-applicable categorization of chordal morphology. Rather, it is

---

11. This classification, rooted in traditional tonal theory, is also supported by experimental studies of tonal perception, e.g., Bingham 1910, Krumhansl 1990.

I assume that—other things being equal—a tonic note, as the point of reference within the tonal system (and, to a lesser degree, the other members of the tonic triad), receives an extra weight, a kind of "tonal emphasis." Thus in examining scale-degree identity I examined whether peaks frequently receive this type of tonal, "grammatical" emphasis. On the other hand, one may hypothesize that peaks, as apexes of tension, would characteristically be associated with instable scale degrees, thus enhancing "rhetorical" emphasis.

12. In the Berg sample, pitch singularity was examined with regard to large sections, for instance, an entire number in *Lulu*.

13. These aspects were investigated in the Haydn and Chopin repertories only. Indeed, some classifications of harmonic structures according to their tensional qualities (e.g., scales of harmonic consonance, such as Helmholz's or Narmour's (1990: 289), or Hindemith's classification of chords) may be applied to both tonal and nontonal contexts. Their application to the study of melodic peaks is not attempted here, however, and may be the subject of a future study.

devised with the specific concerns of this study in mind. Categories were devised primarily to provide information about the association of peaks with specific structures (such as the "dominant" seventh chord), and are particularly related to the biases of tertial harmony and tonal music. Thus, I divided verticalities into six categories: (A) consonant triads—major or minor triads in root position ($\frac{5}{3}$) or in first inversion ($\frac{6}{3}$); (B) major or minor second-inversion ($\frac{6}{4}$) triads; (C) dissonant (diminished and augmented) triads, including all their inversions; (D) major-minor ("dominant") seventh chords; (E) all other seventh chords; and (F) non-tertial verticalities, comprising "non-harmonic" tones (appoggiaturas, suspensions, passing and neighboring tones, etc.). I applied this categorization to verticalities underlining the selected peaks and controls.

Soprano position. The soprano position of a chord designates the interval between its uppermost part and its root (as distinguished from the bass). I examined the soprano position of each selected note, identifying it as the root, the third, the fifth, the seventh or a specific "nonharmonic" tone within its chord.

Dynamics

Dynamic emphasis. To determine whether peaks are associated with dynamic emphasis, I looked for two types of dynamic stress: *processive* stress, the emphasis that a note receives when it is at the apex of a process of dynamic intensification (that is, terminating a *crescendo*); and *local* stress, an abrupt emphasis, at points marked by indications such as *sforzando* or *fp*. The frequency of each of these two types of emphasis at peaks was compared to their frequency in the control group.[14]

Parametric Interaction

Combined parametric emphasis is a summarizing aspect, a rather crude yet useful way of estimating the combined weight of durational, metric, and melodic emphases.[15] It tests the principal hypotheses in another, synoptic way.

After determining whether an examined note is more, less, or equally emphasized in relation to each of its neighbors in these three aspects, I calculated the note's "score," that is, the emphasis resulting from the combined action of the six relations analyzed. If the examined note is emphasized more than one of its neighbors metri-

14. This aspect was not investigated in the early Haydn sample, where dynamic markings are rare.

15. This measure assigns an equal emphatic value to the three examined aspects, ignores other important aspects of emphasis, and disregards the degree of emphasis in each aspect. For these reasons, it is not appropriate as a general measure of emphasis, or for use in critical analyses of specific pieces. The "medium-low" grading of the peak in Example 2.8 (see Table 2.3) is an instance in which this method is misleading. I do believe, however, that it is appropriate in the statistical analysis of a large number of cases.

EXAMPLE 2.5. Chopin, Mazurka in G minor, Opus 24 No. 1, measures 1–8.

cally, durationally, or melodically, one point was added to its score for each parameter. If its neighbor is emphasized, one point is subtracted; and if neither the selected note nor its neighbor is emphasized, no points were added or subtracted. I grouped the scores into four categories: *high emphasis* (4 to 6 points), *medium-high emphasis* (1 to 3 points), *medium-low emphasis* (minus 2 to 0 points) and *low emphasis* (minus 6 to minus 3 points). Thus, the peak in Example 2.8, which is melodically emphasized relative to both its neighbors (2 points), deemphasized metrically (minus 2 points) and equally emphasized durationally (0 points), receives a score of medium-low emphasis (0 points).

If peaks are, indeed, loci of emphasis, the scores for the peaks should be significantly higher than those of the controls. Specifically, there should be significantly more peak notes in the "high emphasis" category, and fewer in the "low emphasis" category.

Interparametric congruence. As already mentioned, for each category of emphasis—durational, metric, and melodic (intervallic)—I determined whether the selected note is more, less, or equally emphasized in relation to its immediate neighbors. For instance, in Example 2.5 the peak, G^5 (measure 4), is metrically more emphasized, but durationally less emphasized than both surrounding notes ($F\sharp^5$ and D^5). Meter and duration are in this case *noncongruent* with each other, the first emphasizing the peak, the second deemphasizing it. Such clashes between emphases in different parameters may enhance tension. Thus it seems possible that interparametric noncongruence would be associated with peaks.

Interparametric *congruence* exists when, in a pair of adjacent notes, the same note is emphasized by the two aspects compared (duration and meter, duration and

EXAMPLE 2.6A. Congruence of emphasis at the peak

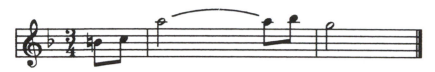

EXAMPLE 2.6B. Congruent attenuation of the peak.

EXAMPLE 2.6C. Parametric noncongruence at the peak.

"melody" (intervallic distance), or meter and melody). In contrast, *noncongruence* exists when each of the two compared parameters emphasizes a different note in the pair.[16] In Example 2.6a all three aspects of emphasis are congruent: the peak, A^5, is emphasized metrically, durationally, and melodically (i.e., by a relatively large intervallic approach). The three parameters are also congruent in Example 2.6b. But instead of strengthening the peak (as in Example 2.6a) duration, meter, and melody combine to weaken it. That is: the peak is shorter, weaker metrically, and weaker melodically than its neighbors, which are preceded by larger intervals.

Example 2.6c illustrates *noncongruence* between durational and metric emphases, and between metric and melodic emphasis. The peak, $B\flat^5$, is emphasized metrically but deemphasized durationally and melodically relative to both its neighbors, A^5 and E^5.

Note that for a selected note, each of the interparametric relations was examined twice: in relation both to its earlier neighbor and to its later neighbor. The two relations are not necessarily the same. In Example 2.7, for example, a metric-durational noncongruence occurs between the peak note (E^5) and its earlier neighbor, C^5, because the peak is emphasized durationally but undermined metrically. In the relation between the peak and its *later* neighbor, D^5, however, meter and duration are congruent: the peak note is emphasized both durationally and metrically.

16. In some cases neither note is emphasized with regard to one or both of the aspects being compared (i.e., they are equal in duration, are equally emphasized metrically, or are approached by the same interval). Such cases, which present neither strong congruence nor forceful noncongruence, have not been included in the congruence statistics.

EXAMPLE 2.7. Interparametric congruence: different relations to
earlier and later neighbors.

TABLE 2.1

	Durational emphasis				Metric emphasis	
	A	B			A	B
+	100	50		+	100	50
−	0	50		−	0	50

TABLE 2.2

	Meter						
Duration	Group A				Group B		
	+	−			+	−	
+	100 (100)	0 (0)	100		50 (25)	0 (25)	50
−	0 (0)	0 (0)	0		0 (25)	50 (25)	0
	100	0	100		50	50	100

For a meaningful statistical analysis of interparametric congruence, it is not enough to compare the frequencies of congruence and noncongruence in different groups (e.g., peaks versus controls). It is also necessary to ascertain whether these frequencies deviate significantly from frequencies expected (given the results in each parameter) from a random interaction between parameters. A significant deviation from expected frequency (EFr) demonstrates that the two parameters are not independent but tend toward congruence or noncongruence.

Consider a hypothetical example. Durational and metric emphases were examined in two groups of melodic peaks, A and B, each composed of 100 notes. The results are presented in Table 2.1. All notes in group A were emphasized (+), while in group B only half (50) of the examined notes were emphasized. This was the case for both durational and metric emphases. Table 2.2 examines durational-metric congruence in the two hypothetical groups. In this table (and in the other congruence tables in this study) congruence figures are indicated by the juncture of the plus row and column, and at the juncture of the minus row and column. Noncongruence figures appear at the juncture of the plus row and minus column, and of the minus row and plus column. Expected frequencies appear in parentheses.

In both groups meter is always congruent with duration: whenever an examined note is longer than its neighbor, it is also emphasized metrically (pluses—top rows, left columns—in Table 2.2), and whenever it is deemphasized durationally, it is also deemphasized metrically (minuses—bottom rows, right columns). However, because results in the compared parameters (meter and duration) are very different in the two groups, this similarity is misleading. All notes were found to be emphasized both metrically and durationally in group A. Consequently, it is inevitable—and uninformative—that metric and durational emphases in this group are always congruent with one another. In group B, on the other hand, only half of the notes were durationally emphasized, and the same was the case for metric emphasis. If the two parameters are independent of one another, one would expect that about half of the notes in this group would exhibit metric-durational congruence (i.e., that approximately half [25] of the durationally emphasized notes would also be metrically emphasized, and about half [25] of the notes deemphasized durationally would be deemphasized metrically as well). The fact that meter and duration are always congruent in group B is thus very informative: it indicates that metric-durational congruence is an independent factor in this group, a factor that cannot be deduced from the frequency of emphasis in each of the two parameters.

My analyses, then, determine for peak and control groups both the actual frequencies of congruence between each two parameters, and the expected ones. A chi-square test for independence was used to determine whether the observed frequency significantly deviates from the expected one. In the case of the control group, such analysis indicates whether certain interparametric congruencies (e.g., between metric accent and durational emphasis) are normative in the repertory as a whole, and these findings make it possible to determine whether such norms are weakened or strengthened at peaks.

Special Cases

Repeated notes. When a peak or control note is repeated several times in succession, I used the following analytic procedure. With respect to metric location, I considered only the first and the last attacks in the series (each of them receives half a point in the statistics). In determining metric and durational emphases I compared the first note in the series, metrically and durationally, with the preceding one, and the last note with the note following it. When examining intervals and melodic emphasis, I ignored the primes between the repeated notes, and considered the intervals preceding and following the group of repeated notes.

"Dead" intervals. It is commonly suggested that intervals following strong closure—so-called "dead" intervals—do not form part of the melodic process because they are not perceived as a part of the intervallic succession of the melodic line. For instance, a wide skip that separates major sections of a piece does not convey the tension conveyed by such a skip in the midst of a phrase. In this study, I ac-

EXAMPLE 2.8. Chopin, Mazurka in G Minor, Opus 67 No. 2, measures 1–16.

cept this notion, but apply it cautiously. Only intervals that immediately follow a formal closure of a section larger than a phrase and a strong harmonic closure (such as an authentic cadence) were considered "dead." Such intervals (very few in the present sample) were omitted from the intervallic statistics, and their relations with surrounding intervals were not considered in determining melodic emphasis.

Change of harmony. When an examined note is harmonized by several different chords, I counted only the chord whose attack occurs with, or immediately follows, the note's attack.

TABLE 2.3: Features examined in Example 2.8

	Relation with earlier neighbor	Relation with later neighbor
DURATION AND METER		
Durational emphasis	=	=
Metric emphasis	−	−
Metric location	off 2nd beat	
Syncopation	No	
Location	last quarter	
MELODY		
Interval identity	minor tenth	minor second
Melodic emphasis	+	+
Melodic scale-degree	$\hat{3}$	
Repeated pitches	no	
Pitch-register singularity		
In segment:	yes	
In piece:	no	
HARMONY		
Harmonic degree:	I	
Chord structure	class A	
Soprano position	third	
DYNAMIC EMPHASIS	not applicable	
PARAMETRIC INTERACTION		
Combined parametric emphasis	0 (medium-low)	
Interparametric congruence		
Meter-duration	not applicable	
Duration-melody	not applicable	
Meter-melody	noncongruence (−+)	noncongruence (−+)

AN EXAMPLE

To illustrate the analytic procedures used in this study, I apply them to a single example: the peak of the opening section of Chopin's Mazurka in G minor, Opus 67 No. 2 (see Table 2.3 and Example 2.8, m. 14). Below, I briefly describe the application of these procedures to the example.

Duration and meter. The peak is as long as its neighbors (G^4 and A^5, m. 14);

hence, an equal durational emphasis (=) is marked in relation to earlier as well as later neighbor. Metrically, however, both neighbors are more emphasized than the peak; metrical emphasis is thus marked "−" in relation to both. Table 2.3 also marks the peak's metric location, as well as its temporal location in the extracted 16-measure segment, and notes the absence of syncopation at the peak.

Melody. I marked the intervals approaching and following the peak (minor tenth and minor second, respectively.). The interval approaching the peak is larger than those approaching both its earlier neighbor (a minor third) and its later (a minor second); thus, the peak is melodically emphasized (+) in relation to both neighbors. Other melodic features noted include the scale-degree identity of the peak ($\hat{3}$ in G minor), and the absence of successive repetition of the peak ("repeated notes"). Pitch singularity is confirmed for the extracted segment, but not for the piece as a whole: within this segment, the only appearance of $B\flat^5$ is at the peak, but it reappears twice later in the piece (mm. 32, 54).

Harmony. The tonic (I) degree, a G minor chord, underlines the peak ("harmonic degree"). As a consonant root-position triad, this chord is designated to class "A" in the chord structure category. The soprano position of this chord, i.e., the relation of its uppermost note (the peak) to its root, G, is a third position (3).

Dynamics. Though no dynamic change is notated at the peak itself, *forte* (probably marking a dynamic intensification) is marked at the following beat, and may be interpreted as applying to the peak as well. However, because dynamic emphasis at the peak is not unequivocally notated, I did not consider this case in the dynamic emphasis statistics.

Parametric interaction. Meter and melody are noncongruent at the peak of Example 2.8: with regard to both neighbors, the peak is emphasized melodically, but deemphasized metrically. Because of the equal emphasis in duration, the durational-metric and durational-melodic congruences are not applicable to this example (see footnote 16).

The computation of the combined parametric emphasis score for this example is described on p. 26 above.

In this chapter I have described a method enabling an investigation of the relationships of contour peaks to other aspects of musical organization, and thus an empirical examination of the hypotheses suggested in Chapter 1. The results of this examination, as applied to three diverse musical repertories, are presented in the following chapters. The next chapter, which applies this method to an early Classic repertory, demonstrates at least one merit of such an empirical approach: though seemingly tedious, it may bear some unexpected results.

CHAPTER 3

Peaks in Haydn:
The Attenuation of Climax

The first body of music analyzed includes works of the young Haydn, written before his move to Eszterháza in 1766.[1] Though clearly the output of an accomplished composer, this music is not characterized by the *Sturm und Drang* expressiveness of Haydn's music in the 1770s, or the mature personal assimilation of Classic idioms found in his late oeuvre. Rather, it is typical of the stylistic trends—principally Viennese and Italian—of the period and provides a good example of *Galant* idioms prevalent in the third quarter of the century.

I included both instrumental and vocal pieces in the Haydn sample: minuet and trio movements from the early keyboard sonatas, nos. 1–18, and two early operas, *Acide* (1763) and *La Canterina* (1766).[2] Genre and medium of performance, however, did not prove to be significant factors in the treatment of peaks in this repertory. I

1. Haydn's move to Eszterháza in 1766 is considered the beginning of a new period in his composition, marked by strong *Sturm und Drang* tendencies (see Larsen 1980: 351–53). I chose to concentrate on pieces written before this stylistic break.

2. The keyboard (probably harpsichord) pieces, all composed before 1766, are sonata-divertimenti in the Viennese tradition, influenced in particular by Wagenseil's divertimenti (see Brown 1986: 179–95; Landon and Jory 1988: 68–70). Many of them are presumed to be didactic pieces written for Haydn's keyboard students, and thus present in an uncomplicated form important idioms of the period. The minuet and trio movements surveyed here usually precede the final movement in these sonatas.

I selected minuet and trio movements in order to compare metric relationships in this repertory with the triple-meter dance movements in the Chopin repertory. Another reason for the selection is the climactic function that they (in particular their trios) often have in Haydn's early sonatas (see Brown: 276).

The two operas were among the first staged for the Esterházy court. *Acide* (only portions of which have survived) is a *festa teatrale* based on the pastoral myth of Acis and Galatea. *La Canterina* is Haydn's earliest surviving Italian opera. It is an *opera buffa*, setting a libretto from an *intermezzo* by Piccinni, concerning a devious young singer and her two suitors (see also Landon and Jory 1988: 60–68, 121–36).

TABLE 3.1. Durational emphasis

	Peaks		Controls	
	%	n	%	n
RELATION WITH EARLIER NEIGHBOR				
+	20	(22)	19	(22)
=	52.7	(56)	62.9	(75)
−	27.3	(32)	18.1	(21)
Total n		118		110
RELATION WITH LATER NEIGHBOR				
+	28.8	(34)	24.1	(28)
=	57.6	(68)	56.9	(66)
−	13.6	(16)	19	(22)
Total n		118		116

found only a few marginally significant differences between these disparate genres (see Eitan 1991, vol. 2, app. 4), and it is likely that the trends found here are generally representative of Haydn's style in this period.

The ensuing analysis reveals that melodic peaks in this early Classic repertory are very different from the intensifying, emphatic phenomenon suggested by my initial hypotheses. Peaks were not generally associated with emphatic, intensifying, or tensional features, and in most respects were not significantly different from controls. Only two emphatic tendencies seem to be characteristic of peaks in this repertory: their frequent association with large intervals, and the inclination to avoid recurrence of the peak pitch. Most of the other durational, metric, and harmonic aspects examined do not significantly emphasize or intensify peaks; indeed, they often seem to attenuate them.

DURATIONAL AND METRIC RELATIONSHIPS

Neither durational nor metric emphasis strongly distinguishes melodic peaks in the Haydn repertory. Hypotheses concerning the temporal location of peaks were not substantiated either.

Durational emphasis (Table 3.1). The tendency to emphasize peaks durationally is weak in this repertory, and applies only to the relation of peaks to their later neighbors (Table 3.1b). There is no significant difference ($p > .05$)[3] between the peaks and

3. Lower case p designates the "level of significance" of the result. The level of significance of a given result is the probability that the null hypothesis (in our case, the hypothesis that the compared

TABLE 3.2. Metric location

Location	Peaks (n=118)		Controls (n=119)	
	%	n	%	n
On beats	54.2	(64)	49.2	(58.5)
On 1st beat	15.7	(18.5)	18.5	(22)
On other beats	38.5	(45.5)	30.7	(36.5)
Off beats	46.8	(54)	50.8	(60.5)
Total n (on+off beats)		118		119

TABLE 3.3. Metric emphasis

	Peaks		Controls	
	%	n	%	n
RELATION WITH EARLIER NEIGHBOR				
+	30.9	(34)	38.8	(45)
=	19.1	(21)	16.4	(19)
−	50	(55)	44.8	(52)
Total n		110		116
RELATION WITH LATER NEIGHBOR				
+	55.1	(65)	48.3	(56)
=	14.4	(17)	14.7	(17)
−	30.5	(36)	37	(43)
Total n		118		116

controls with respect to relations with either earlier or later neighbors. However, testing the null hypothesis (H0) that the proportions (P) of emphasized and deemphasized peaks are equal (H0: P(plus) = P(minus)) presents marginally significant results with regard to relations with later neighbors ($\chi^2 = 5.01$, $p < .05$).

Metric location (Table 3.2). I found no substantial difference in metric location between the peaks and controls ($\chi^2 = 2.1$, $p > .05$). The location of peaks along the metric "grid" is no different from that of other notes, and there is no significant tendency for peaks to occur on metric accents.

Metric emphasis (Table 3.3). Like the metric location statistics, this aspect shows that metric accentuation is not an important feature of peaks in the Haydn

populations, peaks and control, are not different from each other with respect to the examined variable) is true. Usually (at least in research in the social and human sciences) if this probability is smaller than 5 percent ($p < .05$) the null hypotheses is rejected, and the result is accepted as statistically significant.

TABLE 3.4. Syncopation

	Peaks (n=119)		Controls (n=119)	
	%	n	%	n
Syncopated	6.7	(8)	10.1	(12)
Not syncopated	93.3	(111)	89.9	(107)

EXAMPLE 3.1. Haydn, Sonata No. 3 in F Major, Hob. XVI/9, Minuet, measures 11–14.

repertory: peaks are not significantly different from controls with regard to either neighbor ($p > .05$). A marginally significant tendency to emphasize peaks, however, was found in testing the null hypothesis H0: P(plus) = P(minus) for peaks' relations with later neighbors ($\chi^2 = 4.55$, $p < .05$). In contrast, a marginally significant tendency ($.05 < p < .1$) to *de*emphasize peaks metrically applies to their relation to earlier neighbors. This tendency is particularly manifest in the instrumental repertory ($p < .01$). Indeed, in many of the minuets peaks are consistently positioned in unaccented positions (see Examples 3.1–3.3, 3.8–3.11).

Syncopation (Table 3.4). The peaks and controls show no significant difference in frequency of syncopation ($z = 1.28$; $p > .05$).

Three conclusions emerge from this survey of rhythm and meter:

1. Neither durational nor metric accent emphasizes melodic peaks in the Haydn repertory. Rather, these factors often attenuate the effect of a conspicuous contour peak. For instance, in Examples 3.1–3.3 from the minuets, the peaks' emphatic effect (often enhanced by large leaps to them) is undermined by their unaccented metric location and by the absence of durational emphasis. Example 3.4, a rewriting of Example 3.2 (measures 1–4), negatively demonstrates this effect of meter and duration. Aligning contour with metric and durational emphasis creates here a striking expressive contrast with the original, as well as a marked stylistic shift (the altered example sounds almost like a phrase from a nineteenth-century Italian opera)—all without any change in pitch succession.

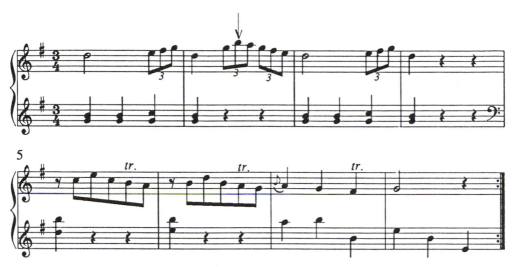

EXAMPLE 3.2. Haydn, Sonata No. 4 in G Major, Hob. XVI/G1, Minuet, measures 1–8.

EXAMPLE 3.3. Haydn, Sonata no. 16 in D Major, Hob. XVI/14, Minuet, measures 29–37.

2. Most peaks (especially in the instrumental sample) are undistinguished from their neighbors in duration, forming a part of a chain of eighth or quarter notes. Embedding peaks within such passages (as illustrated by Examples 3.1–3.3) considerably attenuates their salience.

3. Haydn frequently undermines the emphatic potential of peaks by placing them next to a metrically or durationally emphasized note. The widespread use of this

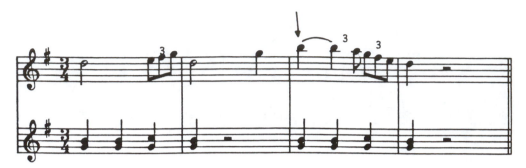

EXAMPLE 3.4. A rewriting of Example 3.2, measures 1–4.

EXAMPLE 3.5. Haydn, Sonata No.12 in A Major, Hob. XVI/12, Minuet, measures 17–24.

strategy shows up in the large number of peaks unemphasized durationally and metrically relative to earlier neighbors (Tables 3.1, 3.3). Examples 3.5 and 3.6 are typical of the instrumental sample, while Example 3.7 demonstrates the use of this strategy in the vocal sample. In these examples (and in many similar cases[4]) the contourally emphasized peak is counter-balanced by the metrically or durationally accented note that precedes it. Thus, meter and duration detract from the force of contour, while contour weakens metric and durational accentuation, creating a complex, delicate balance of emphases.

Often this strategy shapes not only major highpoints but also the smallest melodic units. In Example 3.6 the peaks of most melodic figures immediately follow the downbeat (E$\flat^5$, measure 1; A$\flat^5$, measure 2; B$\flat^5$, measure 3; A$\flat^4$, measure 5; A$\flat^4$,

---

4. Compare, for instance, Examples 3.8 and 3.9 with similar gestures at the Minuets of Sonatas no. 7, Hob. XVII/D1, measures 6 and 13, and Sonata no. 17, Hob. deest, measures 5 and 21.

EXAMPLE 3.6. Haydn, Sonata no. 18 in E♭ Major, Hob. Deest, Minuet, measures 1–8.

EXAMPLE 3.7. Haydn, *La Canterina*, "Che visino delicato," measures 20–24.

measure 7; melodic figures are denoted by brackets). Thus emphasis created by large leaps toward peaks is repeatedly undermined by the preceding metric accent.

Temporal location (Table 3.5). The hypothesis that peaks are normally located in the late portions of segments, one of the frequent claims for melodic contour, is not generally true in the Haydn repertory. A chi-square analysis indicates no significant difference between peaks and controls with regard to location. This holds both for smaller segments, such as eight-measure periods ($\chi^2 = 4.84$; $p > .05$) and for larger segments ($\chi^2 = 5.28$; $p > .05$).[5] Though a standard-score test suggests a tendency to

5. Because most pieces analyzed in the Haydn sample are short, I considered only two levels of segmentation.

TABLE 3.5. Temporal location

	Peaks (n=119)		Controls (n=119)	
	%	n*	%	n
LOWER LEVEL				
1st quarter	22.7	(27)	31.9	(38)
1st note	3.4	(4)	2.5	(3)
2nd quarter	19.9	(23.7)	22.7	(27)
3rd quarter	40.3	(48)	27.7	(33)
Last quarter	17.1	(20.3)	17.6	(21)
Last note	0		.8	(1)
1st half	42.6	(50.7)	55.5	(66)
2nd half	57.4	(68.3)	44.5	(53)
Outer half (1st + last q.)	39.8	(47.3)	49.6	(59)
Inner half (2nd + 3rd q.)	60.2	(71.7)	50.4	(60)
HIGHER LEVEL				
1st quarter	24	(28.5)	23.5	(28)
1st note	2.5	(3)	2.5	(3)
2nd quarter	21.8	(25.9)	27.7	(33)
3rd quarter	34.4	(41)	27.7	(33)
Last quarter	19.8	(23.6)	21	(25)
Last note	0		0	
1st half	45.8	(54.4)	51.2	(61)
2nd half	54.2	(64.6)	48.8	(58)
Outer half (1st + last q.)	44.2	(52.2)	44.6	(53)
Inner half (2nd + 3rd q.)	55.8	(66.8)	55.4	(66)

*Fractions result from cases in which the peak's phrase returns several times in different temporal locations. In the statistical analysis, fractions were rounded to the nearest whole number.

position peaks within the third quarter of periods, this tendency is only marginally significant ($z = 2.05, p < .05$).

The rejection of the "late peak hypothesis" is important, because this hypothesis stems from the image of the "dynamic curve," where the high point of intensity (and correspondingly the melodic peak, one of its major determinants) occurs late in a piece or segment. While the results do not negate the existence of such intensity curves, they do suggest that in the examined Haydn repertory these processes are shaped primarily by domains (such as tonal structure) that are perhaps less direct and "natural" than melodic contour.[6]

6. The fact that "late peaks" are not characteristic of this repertory may be related to the trochaic view of accent—namely, that accent should be placed at the beginning of a segment—a view character-

TABLE 3.6. Intervals

| | Approaching interval | | | | Following interval | | | |
| | Peaks (n=109) | | Controls (n=115) | | Peaks (n=118) | | Controls (n=116) | |
	%	n	%	n	%	n	%	n
Seconds	25.7	(28)	59.1	(68)	39.8	(47)	57.8	(67)
Thirds	20.2	(22)	19.1	(22)	20.3	(24)	21.6	(25)
Perfect fourth	11.9	(13)	7.8	(9)	15.3	(18)	7.8	(9)
Diminished fifth	.9	(1)	.9	(1)	2.5	(3)	2.6	(3)
Perfect fifth	8.3	(9)	5.2	(6)	5.1	(6)	4.3	(5)
Sixths	16.5	(18)	6.1	(7)	11.9	(14)	4.3	(5)
Sevenths	3.7	(4)	.9	(1)	.9	(1)		(0)
Octave	11	(12)	.9	(1)	4.2	(5)	1.7	(2)
>Octave	1.8	(2)		(0)		(0)		(0)
All disjunct	74.3	(81)	40.9	(47)	60.2	(71)	42.2	(49)
>Perfect fifth	33	(36)	7.8	(9)	17	(20)	6	(7)

MELODIC RELATIONSHIPS

Peaks are distinguished in the Haydn repertory mainly by their intervallic relationships and tonal status: intervallically, by a marked tendency to approach and leave peaks by relatively large skips; tonally, by significant association with the submediant (sixth) degree of the prevailing tonality.

Intervals (Table 3.6). There is a highly significant difference ($\chi^2 = 33.28$, $p < .001$) between the peaks and controls in the intervals that approach them. Disjunct intervals ($z = 5.06$, $p < .001$), particularly those larger than a perfect fifth ($z = 4.67$; $p < .001$)—specifically sixths ($z = 2.48$, $p < .05$) and octaves ($z = 3.07$, $p < .01$)—are considerably more frequent in approaches to peaks.

Peaks and controls are also significantly different ($\chi^2 = 10.36$, $p < .01$) in the intervals following them (see Table 3.6, right columns). Again, disjunct intervals ($z = 2.77$, $p < .01$), particularly intervals larger than a perfect fifth ($z = 2.6$, $p < .01$), are significantly more frequent for the peaks. Perfect fourths ($p < .05$) and sixths ($z = 2.05$, $p < .05$) are often associated with descents from peaks.

Separate comparisons of *ascending and descending intervals* also show a highly significant difference between peaks and controls (Table 3.7). The distribution of

istic of the eighteenth century (see Ratner 1982: 192, who quotes Türk in this respect). Placing a melodic peak—an emphasizing agent—near the end of a segment would attenuate trochaic emphasis. In contrast to eighteenth century views, nineteenth-century theorists (such as Riemann) see accent as primarily iambic. As the next chapters will show, the location of peaks the nineteenth- and twentieth-century repertories examined here may reflect this view.

TABLE 3.7. Ascending and Descending Intervals

Intervals	Peaks—ascending (n=109)		Controls—ascending (n=115)		Peaks—descending (n=118)		Controls—descending (n=116)	
	%	n	%	n	%	n	%	n
Seconds	25.7	(28)	55.7	(64)	39.8	(47)	61.2	(71)
Thirds	20.2	(22)	17.4	(20)	20.3	(24)	22.4	(26)
Perfect fourth	11.9	(13)	13	(15)	15.3	(18)	3.4	(4)
Dminished fifth	.9	(1)	3.5	(4)	2.5	(3)	0	(0)
Perfect fifth	8.3	(9)	2.6	(3)	5.1	(6)	6.9	(8)
Sixths	16.5	(18)	5.2	(6)	11.9	(14)	5.2	(6)
Sevenths	3.7	(4)	0	(0)	.9	(1)	.9	(1)
Octave	11	(12)	2.6	(3)	4.2	(5)	0	(0)
>Octave	1.8	(2)	0	(0)	0	(0)	0	(0)
All disjunct	74.3	(81)	44.3	(51)	60.2	(71)	38.8	(45)
>Perfect fifth	33	(36)	7.8	(9)	17	(20)	5.9	(7)

ascending intervals approaching peaks is significantly different from those in the controls ($\chi^2 = 30.3$, $p < .001$). In particular, ascending sixths ($z = 2.76$, $p < .01$), octaves ($z = 2.58$, $p < .01$), as well as the entire group of large upward leaps (ascending intervals larger than a perfect fifth; $z = 4.67$, $p < .001$) are significantly more frequent at peaks.

The distribution of intervals descending from peaks also differs significantly from that of descending intervals in the controls ($\chi^2 = 13.04$, $p < .01$). Disjunct descents in general ($z = 3.29$, $p < .001$), and specifically descents larger than a perfect fifth ($z = 2.61$, $p < .01$), are significantly more frequent at peaks. Like the general intervallic statistics, the comparison of descending intervals indicates that descents of perfect fourths ($z = 3.13$, $p < .002$) and sixths ($z = 1.86$, $p < .05$) are particularly common at peaks.

The interval distribution around peaks is striking. Melodic interval distribution has been studied in diverse Western and non-Western repertories (see, e.g., Watt 1923; Ortmann 1926, 1937; Vos and Troost 1989). These studies show that a higher frequency of smaller intervals, particularly a marked preference for conjunct intervals (also characteristic of the controls), is a near-universal phenomenon, crossing boundaries of time and culture. Similarly, studies of melodic expectancy (Carlsen 1981) have shown that, when asked to continue two-note segments (comprising all intervals up to an octave), in most cases subjects from diverse cultural backgrounds provided a conjunct continuation. Thus, interval distribution around peaks in Haydn (and, as I later demonstrate, in other repertories) deviates markedly not only from a stylistic norm, but possibly also from a universal melodic constraint.

EXAMPLE 3.8. Haydn, Sonata No. 2 in C Major, Hob. XVI/7, Minuet, measures 9–12.

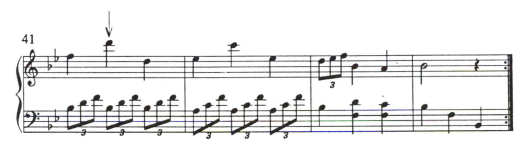

EXAMPLE 3.9. Haydn, Sonata No. 3 in F Major, Hob. XVI/9, Minuet, measures 41–45.

However, while peaks in the Haydn repertory are unequivocally distinguished by intervallic configuration, such configurations are usually used in ways that prevent exaggerated emphasis.

Most peaks that are approached by a large leap are also left by a leap, sometimes equally large, rather than by a disjunct descent. Such two-leap patterns are more common here than "prototypic" tension-release melodic formations, such as "gap-fill" structures, that have often been related to melodic peaks.[7]

Frequently, these two-leap patterns are arppeggiation figures. Because these arppeggiations do not involve any harmonic change, they are not highly emphatic or tensional (rather, an unusually wide arppeggiation often creates a somewhat playful impression). Examples 3.8 and 3.9 are two instances of this gesture, particularly common in the instrumental sample.

Further, such peaks are often embedded within bilinear melodic patterns, where a single part presents two registrally separated melodic strata. For instance, though the D^6 peak in Example 3.8 is immediately approached by a leap of a sixth from F^5,

7. In a gap-fill schema, a disjunct interval (in the present context, the leap preceding the peak) creates a "gap" by skipping over intervening scale degrees. This gap is later filled by conjunct intervals in the opposite direction—the "fill" part of the schema. The gap in a gap-fill structure creates a tension-raising implication for its fill; the ensuing conjunct fill realizes this implication, and thus relieves tension. Gap-fill structures are discussed by Leonard B. Meyer, who coined the term for this pattern (1956: 134ff; 1973: 145–57).

TABLE 3.8. Melodic emphasis

	Peaks		Controls	
	%	n	%	n
RELATION WITH EARLIER NEIGHBOR				
+	61.8	(63)	36.7	(40)
=	8.8	(9)	29.4	(32)
−	29.4	(30)	33.9	(37)
Total n		102		109
RELATION WITH LATER NEIGHBOR				
+	46.8	(51)	33.9	(38)
=	24.8	(27)	28.6	(32)
−	28.4	(31)	37.5	(42)
Total n		109		112

it is also connected linearly with C^6, the highpoint of the preceding measure (while the F^5 approaching the peak forms a part of the lower line G–F–E, connecting the downbeats of measures 9–11). Such near-surface linear connections may detract from the emphatic and intensifying impact of an immediate approach by large leaps.

Lastly, most peaks that are approached by wide leaps are relatively unaccented metrically. This trait is chiefly associated with the instrumental sample, where peaks approached by a sixth, for instance, are invariably unaccented relative to the note preceding them (as in Examples 3.8 and 3.9).

Melodic emphasis (Table 3.8). There is a significant difference between peaks and controls in melodic emphasis in relation to earlier neighbors ($\chi^2 = 18.31$; $p < .001$), but not in relation to later neighbors ($\chi^2 = 3.94$; $p > .05$). This difference between neighbors reflects the tendency to follow, as well as approach, peaks with large intervals (the "relation with later neighbor" category compares the interval approaching an examined note with the one following it).

Scale degree (Table 3.9). Peaks and controls show a significant difference ($\chi^2 = 21.15$, $p < .01$) in the distribution of melodic scale degrees (as determined in relation to the local tonic). This difference arises chiefly from differences in the frequency of two degrees: $\hat{6}$ is significantly more frequent for the peaks, ($z = 3.7$, $p < .001$), while $\hat{7}$ is considerably less frequent there ($z = 2.54$, $p < .02$).

I found no significant difference between peaks and controls when scale-degree identity was related to the pieces' principal tonic ($\chi^2 = 8.81$, $p > .05$).

The absence of scale degree $\hat{7}$ at peaks is hardly surprising, given the tendency of leading notes to move toward the higher tonic note. The use of scale degree $\hat{6}$ as a peak, however, calls for further examination, because it seems to point at an un-

TABLE 3.9. Scale degree

	Relation to local tonality				Relation to principal tonality			
	Peaks (n=118)		Controls (n=119)		Peaks (n=102)		Controls (n=103)	
	%	n	%	n	%	n	%	n
$\hat{1}$	19.5	(23)	18.5	(22)	21.6	(22)	20.9	(21.5)
$\hat{2}$	12.3	(14.5)	13.9	(16.5)	8.3	(10.5)	16.5	(17)
$\hat{3}$	9.3	(11)	13.9	(16.5)	9.8	(10)	13.6	(14)
$\hat{4}$	15.3	(18)	19.7	(23.5)	11.8	(12)	12.1	(12.5)
$\hat{5}$	19.5	(23)	19.7	(23.5)	18.1	(18.5)	21.4	(22)
$\hat{6}$	22.9	(27)	5.9	(7)	23.5	(24)	7.8	(8)
$\hat{7}$	1.3	(1.5)	8.4	(10)	6.9	(7)	7.8	(8)
$\hat{1},\hat{3},\hat{5}$	48.3	(57)	52.1	(62)	49.5	(50.5)	52.1	(57.5)
$\hat{1},\hat{5}$	39	(46)	38.2	(45.5)	39.7	(40.5)	41.3	(42.5)

anticipated style-related feature. In most cases, peaks employing scale degree 6 are associated with a specific style structure. This structure, which almost invariably precedes a cadence, often involves a gap-fill configuration, comprising a leap toward the sixth degree peak and a conjunct descent toward a cadential tonic note (or in some cases toward a "half cadence" with the leading note on top). Most often, this descent is composed of equidurational motion in eighth or quarter notes. In nearly all cases the sixth degree peak in such a configuration appears in an offbeat or otherwise unaccented position, a position that strongly undermines its climactic potential. Examples 3.10 and 3.11 present this structure in a direct, unelaborated form, comprising all the characteristics described above: precadential location, gap-fill motion to the tonic, equidurational progression, and an unaccented sixth-degree peak.

The deemphasizing factors associated with such configurations prevent the emergence of a forceful climax at the peak. Rather, the melodic peak seems to function in these style structures (commonplace throughout the Classical period) as a conventional precadential sign, a warning of impending closure (see Meyer 1989: 262). As Chapter 4 demonstrates, this conventional function of melodic peaks in Haydn distinguishes them from the climactic "structural highpoints" common in the music of the nineteenth century.

Repeated pitches (Table 3.10). Repeated-pitch configurations are not significantly associated with peaks in the Haydn repertory.

Pitch-register singularity (Table 3.11). Melodic peaks in the Haydn repertory are frequently unique within a segment or an entire movement. Over two-thirds of the peak pitches do not recur within the period ($z = 8.4$, $p < .0001$). Further, the peaks that do recur mostly appear within an immediate repetition of an entire figure, a pro-

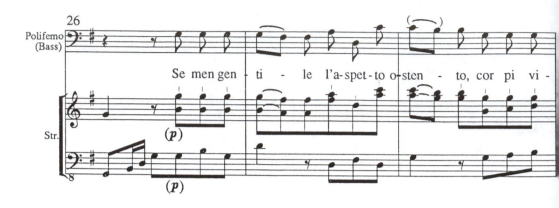

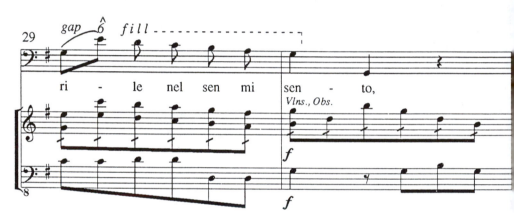

EXAMPLE 3.10. Haydn, *Acide,* "Se men gentile," measures 26–30.

cedure that does not detract from the impression of the peak's uniqueness (see, e.g., Example 3.12, measures 5–8). At a higher level, 20 of the 119 peaks examined—a highly significant frequency, compared to the controls ($z = 3.67$, $p < .001$)—do not recur within the entire movement, except in a context of a repetition of the phrase or period in which they originally appeared, and a significant number of peaks do not recur throughout the entire piece ($z = 2.34$, $p < .05$).

This practice of reserving the peak-pitch for a single appearance is observed not only for strongly emphasized peaks. Even when a peak is seemingly undistinguished—short, unaccented, and without conspicuous intervallic configuration—Haydn guards against obscuring its effect (and thus the effect of the melodic line as a whole) by avoiding its repetition. Perhaps more than any other aspect of the treatment of peaks, the tendency to avoid their repetition suggests that Haydn handles the melodic peak as a special, sensitive locus.

EXAMPLE 3.11. Haydn, Sonata no. 5 in G Major, Hob. XVI/11, Minuet, measures 25–34.

TABLE 3.10. Repeated pitches

	Peaks (n=119)		Controls (n=119)	
	%	n	%	n
Repeated	12.6	(15)	16	(19)
Not repeated	87.4	(104)	84	(100)

TABLE 3.11. Pitch-register singularity

	Peaks (n=119)		Controls (n=119)	
	%	n	%	n
In period	68.1	(81)	14.3	(17)
In movement	16.8	(20)	2.5	(3)
In piece	8.4	(10)	1.7	(2)

Note: singularity counts in movement and piece exclude repetitions of entire phrases

HARMONY

None of the harmonic aspects investigated indicates a preference for tensional entities (such as dissonant chord morphologies) or for syntactically preeminent ones (such as tonic chords). However, chord structure and soprano position exhibit some features significantly associated with peaks.

EXAMPLE 3.12. Haydn, Sonata No. 2 in C Major, Hob. XVI/7, Minuet, measures 1–8.

TABLE 3.12. Harmonic degrees

| Degree | Peaks (n=118) | | Controls (n=119) | |
	%	n	%	n
I	41.5	(49)	39.9	(47.5)
V	28.4	(35.5)	26.9	(32)
Other degrees	30.1	(35.5)	33.2	(39.5)

Harmonic degree (Table 3.12). There is virtually no difference between peaks and controls in the distribution of harmonic degrees ($\chi^2 = .42$, $p > .95$).

Chord structure (Table 3.13). A chi-square analysis indicates that the structure of the chords underlying peaks differs significantly from that of chords in the controls ($\chi^2 = 14.23$, $p < .01$). This result is somewhat misleading, however, because the difference stems from a single tendency: the strong inclination ($z = 3.34$, $p < .001$) to avoid placing peaks over second-inversion ($^6_4$) triads. In all other chord categories, peaks are not significantly different from controls.

Second-inversion triads are avoided at peaks in this repertory because such chords characteristically employ voice-leading in which the upper voice is a passing note, and cannot function as a melodic peak (see, e.g., Example 3.13). Thus, by preventing the occurrence of the dissonant second inversion with a melodic peak, this textbook voice-leading smooths the emphatic effect of the peak in yet another way.

Soprano position (Table 3.14). A chi-square analysis shows no significant difference between peaks and controls as a whole with regard to soprano position ($\chi^2 = 9.14$, $p > .05$). Two slight differences emerge, however: fifth positions are mar-

TABLE 3.13. Chord structure

	Peaks (n=118)		Controls (n=115)	
	%	n	%	n
a. Major or minor triads, $\frac{5}{3}$ or $\frac{6}{3}$	65.3	(77)	60.9	(70)
b. Major or minor $\frac{6}{4}$ triads	0		8.7	(10)
c. Diminished or augmented triads	4.2	(5)	6.7	(8)
d. "Dominant" seventh chords	18.6	(22)	11.3	(13)
e. Other seventh chords	3.4	(4)	1.7	(2)
f. All other verticalities	8.5	(10)	10.4	(12)
d+e. (all seventh chords)	22	(26)	13	(15)
b+f[8]	8.5	(10)	19.1	(22)

EXAMPLE 3.13. Haydn, Sonata No. 4 in G Major,
Hob. XVI/G1, Minuet, measures 7–8.

ginally more frequent at peaks ($z = 2.32$, $p < .05$), and octave positions at the controls ($z = 2.04$, $p < .05$). The high frequency of fifth positions may simply stem from a preference for "root" arpeggiations of triads (e.g., $\hat{1}$–$\hat{3}$–$\hat{5}$) over "inverted" ones (e.g., ascending $\hat{3}$–$\hat{5}$–$\hat{8}$ or $\hat{5}$–$\hat{8}$–$\hat{3}$), a preference that would frequently engender fifth position peaks.

PARAMETRIC INTERACTION

None of the parametric interactions studied exhibits a significant difference between peaks and controls.

Combined parametric emphasis (Table 3.15). This summarizing aspect clearly shows that peaks are not strongly emphasized in the Haydn repertory. The distribution of the four degrees of combined emphasis is not significantly different in the peaks

---

8. This category is based on the conception of $\frac{6}{4}$ chords as resulting primarily from contrapuntal progressions involving "nonharmonic" tones, such as suspensions or passing notes.

TABLE 3.14. Soprano positions

	Peaks (n=118)		Controls (n=110)	
	%	n	%	n
CHORDAL TONES	91.6	(108)	90	(100)
3	16.1	(19)	24.5	(27)
5	39	(46)	24.5	(27)
8	26.3	(31)	39.1	(43)
7	10.2	(12)	7.3	(8)
NON-CHORD TONES	8.4	(10)	9	(10)
6 (13)	5.9	(7)	1.8	(2)
9	1.7	(2)	3.6	(4)
11	8	(1)	3.6	(4)

TABLE 3.15. Combined parametric emphasis

	Peaks (n=119)		Controls (n=119)	
	%	n	%	n
High (4–6)	10.9	(13)	8.4	(10)
Medium-high (1–3)	39.5	(47)	36.1	(43)
Medium-low (−2–0)	37.8	(45)	39.5	(47)
Low (−6–−3)	11.8	(14)	16	(19)

and controls ($\chi^2 = 1.37, p > .05$). "High emphasis" is not significantly more frequent at peaks, nor is "low emphasis" significantly less frequent. The balancing of melodic emphasis—such as that created by large leaps—by durational or metric deemphasis (see, e.g., Examples 3.1–3.3) is evident in these results: 77.7 percent of the peaks fall within the range of the two "medium emphasis" categories.

Interparametric congruence (Tables 3.16–3.18).[9] Peaks and controls show no significant difference in interparametric congruence. In both groups there is a highly significant tendency for congruence between metric and durational emphasis ($\chi^2 = 36.77, p < .001$ for peaks; $\chi^2 = 21.34, p < .001$ for controls); neither show for congruence between melodic emphasis and either metric emphasis (where $\chi^2 = 1.41, p > .05$ for peaks; $\chi^2 = 1.49, p > .05$ for controls) or durational emphasis ($\chi^2 = 1.56, p > .05$ for peaks; $\chi^2 = .003, p > .95$ for controls).

9. The congruence tables (Tables 3.16–3.18) combine the results regarding relations to earlier and later neighbors. Bracketed numbers are EFrs.

TABLE 3.16. Congruence between durational and metric emphases

Duration	Meter					
	Peaks			Controls		
	+	−		+	−	
+	45 (31.3)	7 (20.7)	52	35 (24.8)	10 (20.2)	45
−	8 (21.7)	28 (14.3)	36	9 (19.2)	26 (15.8)	35
	53	35	88	44	36	80

TABLE 3.17. Congruence between metric and melodic emphases

Meter	Melody					
	Peaks			Controls		
	+	−		+	−	
+	53 (49.6)	25 (28.4)	78	38 (34.5)	28 (31.5)	66
−	38 (41.4)	27 (23.6)	65	31 (34.5)	35 (31.5)	66
	91	52	143	69	63	13

TABLE 3.18. Congruence between durational and melodic emphases

Duration	Melody					
	Peaks			Controls		
	+	−		+	−	
+	34 (31.2)	15 (17.8)	49	18 (17.9)	19 (19.1)	37
−	22 (24.8)	17 (14.2)	39	12 (12.1)	13 (12.9)	25
	56	32	88	30	32	62

CONCLUSION

The hypothesis that peaks are generally related to emphasizing, intensifying, or ten-sional features is not confirmed for Haydn, nor are most of the secondary hypotheses emanating from it. It would be wrong, however, to conclude that contour peaks (and by implication the dimension of melodic contour in general) are inconsequential in this body of music: several dimensions surveyed reveal that peaks are treated differ-ently from other points on the melodic curve, suggesting that melodic contour plays a part in structuring the repertory sampled.

Perhaps the clearest indication of the significance of contour is the marked tendency to avoid repeating peaks within the same phrase or period. This tendency, while it does not point to any specific structural role of peaks, indicates sensitivity to the salience of contour peaks and thus suggests that melodic shape is a substantial aspect of phrase construction in this style. Similarly, the statistically significant associations of peaks with large intervals (in approach and in descent) and with a specific scale degree (the submediant) show that peaks are treated differently from other, less conspicuous points on the melodic curve. Altogether, these tendencies suggest that contour is a consequential compositional dimension in the Haydn repertory.

The results also reveal, however, a tendency to avoid or counterbalance the emphatic or intensifying connotations of contour peaks. Rather than aligning peaks with other emphatic phenomena, such as metric and durational accents (as my principal hypothesis suggested), Haydn frequently associates them with weak metric placement or short duration. He therefore weakens the climactic potential inherent in peaks, thus diminishing the role of contour in shaping mid- and large-scale dynamic curves. The data which indicate that peaks in the Haydn repertory appear near the beginning of segments as often as in their later parts (where the highpoints of dynamic curves are supposed to be located) further support this conclusion.

Why is the climactic potential of melodic peaks unrealized, even inhibited, in the Haydn repertory? A possible explanation may point to the primacy of conventional schemes in this style, which may diminish the significance of universal phenomena such as melodic peaks. Because conventional melodic formulae and formal designs, conjoined with the syntax of harmony and voice leading, clearly delineate structure in most of the examined pieces, the more "natural" dimensions, such as melodic contour, might be less necessary in shaping major structural processes. Further, frequent highly emphatic, climactic peaks may be inappropriate to the reserved, aristocratic *Galant* idiom that characterizes many of the Haydn pieces surveyed, the minuets in particular. We may get an image of *Galant* expressive mores, and possibly a notion of their melodic implications, by the following excerpt from a contemporary Viennese criticism of Haydn's music:[10]

> Herr Joseph Hayden [*sic*], the darling of our nation, whose gentle character impresses itself on each of his pieces. His movements have beauty, order, clarity, a fine and noble expression. . . . In his cassatios, quartets and trios he is pure and clean water, over which a southerly wind occasionally ripples, and sometimes rises to waves without, however, losing its bed and course . . . and in minuets [he is] natural, playful, alluring.[11]

One can imagine here (particularly in the extended water metaphor), perhaps, not only a figurative evaluation of Haydn's achievements in different genres, but an

10. See, for instance, Brown 1986: 285.
11. "On the Viennese Taste in Music," in the *Wiener Diarium* 1766 (cited by Landon 1978: 130)

illustration of his melodic idiom, specifically his sensitive attenuation of melodic climax. An overdramatic, climactic emphasis of melodic peaks would indeed risk turning Haydn's gentle "southerly wind" into a tempest, thus losing the safety of an alluring, *Galant* cruise. Haydn's careful balancing of melodic emphasis thus neatly demonstrates the *Galant* "nothing in excess" aesthetics.

How, then, do melodic peaks function in this style? First, the need to avoid the "natural" emphasis of contour peaks probably plays a part in shaping Haydn's melodic lines. This may be one reason for the frequent association of peaks with weak metric placement, and for voice leading that prevents the upper notes of tense chords (like cadential second inversion triads) from functioning as contour peaks. Second, while peaks in the Haydn repertory are rarely points of intense climax, they sometimes are part of a conventional sign of approaching harmonic and formal closure. The peak in such situations is not itself a focal point, but a pointer, directing attention toward a structural event. While durational and metric attenuation prevents such pointer peaks from becoming the crux of the musical process, their inherent registral salience functions within a conventional style schema as a forward-pointing sign.

CHAPTER 4

Chopin: Melodic Peaks, Salience, and Intensity

I selected for analysis Chopin's waltzes and mazurkas,[1] two genres that contrast substantially in significant ways: they present disparate rhythmic patterning and, equally important, demonstrate radically different compositional approaches.[2] While some of the generic contrasts are reflected in the treatment of melodic peaks (particularly the tendency to emphasize upbeats in the mazurkas),[3] in most respects results in these

1. I surveyed all the published Chopin waltzes (excluding the spurious KK IVa No. 14), and the first two mazurkas of each opus.

2. An unambiguous metric pattern, established by decisive down-beat stresses, characterizes most of Chopin's waltzes, while second and third beat stresses—often violently disruptive of metric regularity—are a salient feature of his mazurkas.

Equally important, Chopin's waltzes and mazurkas exhibit strikingly different compositional approaches. For Chopin, the mazurkas were a ground for radical experimentation, involving bold uses of chromatic harmony (e.g., in the Mazurka in A Minor, Opus 17 No. 4, or the Mazurka in F Minor, Opus 68 No. 4), and the incorporation of striking folklike characteristics (derived from the mazurka's folk ancestors, the *mazur* and the *kujawiak*). These folk elements include the use of harmonic and melodic modal means (particularly Lydian, as in the Mazurka in C Major, Opus 24 No. 2, or the Mazurka in F Major, Opus 68 No. 3); clashes between metric accent and dynamic stress; extensive use of drone effects; and even radical formal schemes, such as that of the "senza fine" Mazurka, Opus 7 No. 5, which imitates the open-ended continuousness of a folk dance.

Chopin's waltzes, on the other hand, rarely manifest such compositional boldness. In most of the waltzes both tonal language and rhythmic organization are clear and straightforward, without any of the complex and idiosyncratic ambiguity manifest in the mazurkas. When Chopin deviates in the waltzes from the secure path of salon-music, it is mostly in a witty, whimsical manner (as in Opus 34 No. 3, where a continuous clash between a 3/4 accompaniment and stubborn 4/4 figures creates a playful, almost childlike quality). Also see Samson 1985, Chapters 6 and 7.

3. Peaks in the mazurkas appear much more frequently on second and third beats, thus reflecting—and perhaps partly generating—the characteristic accentuation of upbeats in this genre. A comparison of peaks in waltzes and mazurkas appears in Eitan 1991, vol. 2.

diverse bodies of music are surprisingly similar: the Chopin sample as a whole, regardless of genre, exhibits a distinctive handling of peaks, supporting the notion of the melodic peak as a locus of emphasis and intensity.

Chopin's treatment of peaks contrasts sharply with Haydn's. While peaks in the Haydn repertory significantly differ from controls in only a few respects, in Chopin peaks and controls are significantly (and often radically) different in most of the examined features. Unlike Haydn's peaks, Chopin's employ duration, meter, interval size, and dynamics to enhance emphasis; they are associated with harmonic tension; and they often appear late in segments, as postulated by the "dynamic curve" model. Together, these features create a characteristically climactic apex, clearly distinct from the attenuated "pointer" peaks typical of the Haydn repertory.

DURATIONAL AND METRIC RELATIONSHIPS

All aspects of temporal organization examined make it evident that Chopin's exploited the emphatic and climactic potentials of peaks. Melodic peaks in Chopin are often emphasized durationally and metrically; often they appear late in mid-level segments, thus serving as the culmination of a dynamic curve.

Durational emphasis (Table 4.1). The placement of an agogic accent at the melodic peak is clearly a norm in the examined Chopin repertory. Peaks longer than their neighbors are significantly more frequent than shorter peaks ($\chi^2 = 5.12, p < .05$ for earlier neighbors, $\chi^2 = 8.74, p < .01$ for later ones).[4] As expected, no tendency toward durational lengthening is found in the control group, which is indeed significantly different from the peaks in that respect ($\chi^2 = 9.94, p < .01$ for earlier neighbors, $\chi^2 = 13.71, p < .005$ for later ones).

Table 4.1c compares the frequencies of two more specific configurations in peaks and controls: in one (marked + +), the examined note is longer than *both* neighbors, and thus strongly emphasized; in the other (marked = =) a note is not distinguished durationally from its two neighbors, and emphasis is thus undermined. While the attenuating " = = " relationship is considerably less frequent at peaks, the emphasizing "+ +" configuration is three times more frequent for peaks than for the controls ($\chi^2 = 14.14, p < .001$). Examples 4.1 and 4.2 illustrate such strong agogic emphasis at peaks, as do many other highpoints in the waltzes and the mazurkas (e.g. measure 75 in the Waltz in C♯ Minor, Opus 64 No. 2; measure 36 in the Mazurka in C Minor, Opus 30 No. 1; and measures 3–4 in the Mazurka in F Minor, Opus 63 No. 2).

Metric location (Table 4.2). A comparison of peaks and controls indicates a tendency for peaks to occur on metrical accents ($\chi^2 = 14.21, p < .05$). First-beat location is twice as frequent at peaks (42.8% vs. 21%; $p < .001$). Offbeat locations are twice as frequent in the controls (17.5% vs. 34%; $p < .01$).

---

4. These are results of testing H0: P(plus) = P(minus).

TABLE 4.1. Durational emphasis

	Peaks		Controls	
	%	n	%	n
A. RELATION WITH EARLIER NEIGHBOR				
+	45.4	(44)	24	(24)
=	40.2	(39)	56	(56)
−	14.4	(14)	20	(20)
total n		97		100
B. RELATION WITH LATER NEIGHBOR				
+	51.6	(50)	26	(26)
=	35	(34)	51	(51)
−	13.4	(13)	23	(23)
total n		97		100
C. SELECTED RELATIONS WITH BOTH NEIGHBORS				
+ +	39.2	(38)	14	(14)
= =	23.7	(23)	38	(38)

Metric emphasis (Table 4.3). Relative to their neighbors, the majority of the examined peaks are metrically emphasized. Results are significant with respect to the peaks' relation with later neighbors ($z = 2.226, p < .05$, for H0: P(plus) = P(minus)), and highly significant regarding peaks' relation with their earlier neighbors ($\chi^2 = 9.22, p < .001$). Thus, in this repertoire a movement toward a peak is characteristically from a metrically unaccented note to a metrically accented one, and the motion away from the peak is from an accented note to an unaccented one (as in Examples 2.5 and 4.4a).

The contoural emphasis created by peaks thus frequently concurs in Chopin with emphases generated by duration and by meter. The first kind of concurrence is well known, not only from studies of music: the elongation of stressed syllables — which often feature the pitch peak — is a common characteristic of speech, often noted in comparative studies of intonation (Bolinger 1986: 238; Cruttenden 1986: 24, 25). Such elongation provides a well-grounded, "natural" model for concurrence of peaks and durational emphases in music.

The concurrence of contoural and metric emphases is of a particular interest for a different reason. Unlike duration (which is a primary psychoacoustical parameter) meter is an emergent property, arising out of a combination of factors whose identity is still a matter of dispute.[5] The considerable correlation between metric emphasis

5. Notable recent contributions to this ongoing debate include Benjamin 1984; Berry 1985; Lerdahl and Jackendoff 1983; Narmour 1990.

EXAMPLE 4.1. Chopin, Waltz in E♭ Major, Opus 18, measures 117–132.

and melodic peaks in the Chopin repertory suggests that in this style melodic contour plays a part in establishing metric structure. Just as correlation with metric accents strengthens the emphatic potential of melodic peaks, so correlation with peaks (and probably with ascent in general) helps to articulate metric accent.

Syncopation (Table 4.4). Though peaks in Chopin are syncopated more often than controls, the results are not statistically significant ($z = 1.75$, $p > .05$).

Temporal location (Table 4.5). In the Chopin repertory, my hypothesis that peaks

EXAMPLE 4.2. Chopin, Waltz in Db Major, Opus 64 No. 1, measures 1–15.

occur towards the end of a segment applies best to the middle level of segmentation (most often, sixteen-measure periods). At this level, peaks and controls are significantly different ($\chi^2 = 12.16$, $p < .01$). Specifically, peaks tend to be located in the second half and in the last quarter of a segment ($z = 2.64$, $p < .01$). Peaks also appear frequently as the last notes in segments of that size ($z = 3.19$, $p < .002$). In contrast, no significant difference between peaks and controls occurs at lower or higher levels of segmentation. However, peaks frequently occur as the terminal notes of lower-level segments (mostly, eight-measure segments) as well ($z = 3.19$, $p < .002$). Marking ends

TABLE 4.2. Metric location

Location	Peaks (n=97)		Controls (n=100)	
	%	n	%	n
On beats	82.5	(80)	66	(66)
On 1st beat	42.8	(41.5)	21	(21)
On 2nd beat	18	(17.5)	24	(24)
On 3rd beat	21.7	(21)	21	(21)
Off beats	17.5	(17)	34	(34)
Off 1st beat	6.2	(6)	9	(9)
Off 2nd beat	4.6	(4.5)	11.5	(11.5)
Off 3rd beat	6.7	(6.5)	13.5	(13.5)

TABLE 4.3. Metric emphasis

	Peaks		Controls	
	%	n	%	n
RELATION WITH EARLIER NEIGHBOR				
+	62.9	(61)	47	(47)
=	14.4	(14)	10	(10)
−	22.7	(22)	43	(43)
Total n		97		100
RELATION WITH LATER NEIGHBOR				
+	56.7	(55)	48	(48)
=	8.2	(8)	9	(9)
−	35.1	(34)	43	(43)
Total n		97		100

TABLE 4.4. Syncopation

	Peaks (n=97)		Controls (n=100)	
	%	n	%	n
Syncopated	5.2	(5)	1	(1)
Not syncopated	94.8	(92)	99	(99)

TABLE 4.5. Temporal location

Lower level	Peaks (n=96)		Controls (n=100)	
	%	n*	%	n*
1st quarter	19.4	(18.6)	18	(18)
1st note	1.6	(1.5)	0	(0)
2nd quarter	24.6	(23.6)	29	(29)
3rd quarter	27.8	(26.7)	30.5	(30.5)
Last quarter	28.2	(27.2)	22.5	(22.5)
Last note	12.5	(12)	1	(1)
1st half	44	(42.2)	47	(47)
2nd half	56	(53.8)	53	(53)
Outer half (1st + last q.)	47.6	(45.8)	40.5	(40.5)
Inner half (2nd + 3rd q.)	52.4	(50.2)	59.5	(59.5)

Middle level	Peaks (n=87)		Controls (n=93)	
	%	n*	%	n*
1st quarter	13.9	(12.1)	29	(27)
1st note	1.1	(1)	0	(0)
2nd quarter	20.2	17.6	29	(27)
3rd quarter	28.6	26.9	23.7	(22)
Last quarter	37.3	(31.4)	18.3	(17)
Last note	10.1	(8.8)	0	(0)
1st half	33.7	(29.7)	58	(54)
2nd half	66.3	(58.3)	42	(39)
Outer half (1st + last q.)	50.6	(44.5)	47.3	(44)
Inner half (2nd + 3rd q.)	49.4	(43.5)	52.7	(49)

Higher level	Peaks (n=70)		Controls (n=82)	
	%	n*	%	n*
1st quarter	19.4	(12.4)	32.3	(27)
1st note	0		0	
2nd quarter	33.1	(23.7)	30.5	(25)
3rd quarter	24	(16.8)	22	(18)
Last quarter	24.9	(17.3)	14.6	(12)
Last note	1	(0.7)	0	(0)
1st half	51.3	(35.9)	62.7	(52)
2nd half	48.9	(34.1)	36.6	(30)
Outer half (1st + last q.)	42.9	(29.7)	47.5	(40)
Inner half (2nd + 3rd q.)	57.1	(40.5)	52.5	(42)

*See Table 3.5.

of phrases with a salient highpoint thus seems a characteristic Chopinesque melodic gesture.[6]

The tendency for melodic peaks to occur late in midlevel segments is primarily a result of a specific melodic framework that is very common—almost normative—in the examined Chopin repertory. In periodic structure (usually of $8 + 8$ measures), the consequent phrase ascends to a peak higher than that of the antecedent. Such peaks, which often precede a descent to the final cadence in the period, usually coincide with the point of maximum harmonic tension. This elevation of both pitch and harmonic tension strongly marks the final cadence and the consequent phrase as a whole. Together with other aspects, the higher peak thus structurally accents the later segment of the period.[7] This is the case in Example 4.3, in which the concurrence of harmonic intensity (a chromatic shift to V^7 / II, the harmonic "point of farthest remove" in this period), a crescendo, and a melodic peak, creates a local climax of considerable force (measure 92).[8]

The abundance of late climaxes in sixteen-measure periods makes it evident that such segments frequently conform to the "dynamic curve" model, which portrays a process of gradual intensification through most of a unit, followed by a shorter phase of abatement. In periodic structures such as those discussed here, this curve of intensity often consists of a composite of two lower-level curves, the second rising, both in pitch and in a general level of intensity, above the first. It is noteworthy, however, that

6. See, for instance, the Waltz in Ab Major, Opus 34 No. 1, measure 40; the Waltz in F Major, Opus 34 No. 3, measure 32; the Waltz in C♯ Minor, Opus 64 No. 2, measure 48; the Mazurka in A Minor, Opus 41 No. 2, measure 34; the Mazurka in Ab Major, Opus 59 No. 2, measure 3, and the Mazurka in A Minor, Opus 68 No. 2, measure 8.

7. Though precadential peaks are also common in the Haydn repertory (see chapter 3), their functions in the two styles are different. The difference is expressed, among other things, in local aspects of emphasis: in Chopin the precadential peak is typically emphasized durationally, metrically, and dynamically, and often receives yet more stress by functioning as a dissonant appoggiatura. In contrast, the precadential peaks in the Haydn sample are typically attenuated both metrically and durationally and are not significantly associated with dissonances. These local differences are, however, symptomatic of a difference of structural status. While the precadential peaks in Haydn function primarily as local markers, those in Chopin are frequently points of climax, midlevel "structural highpoints" that are the culmination of a gradual build-up, both in register and in other parameters, such as harmonic tension, textural density, or dynamics.

8. Some of numerous other cases of such structures appear in the Waltz in A minor, Opus 34 No. 2, measures 53–68 (peak at measure 66); the Waltz in Db Major, Opus 64 No. 1, measures 21–36 (peak at measure 32), and measures 36–52 (peak at measure 50); the Waltz in C♯ Minor, Opus 64 No. 2 measures 33–48 (peak at measure 48); the Waltz in Ab Major, Opus 64 No. 3, measures 1–16 (peak at measure 13); Waltz in Ab Major, Opus 69 No. 1, measures 1–16 (peak at measure 9); the Waltz in B Minor, Opus 69 No. 2, measures 1–16 (peak at measure 13); the Mazurka in F♯ Minor, Opus 6 No. 1, measures 1–16 (peak at measures 13–15); the Mazurka in Bb Major, Opus 17 No. 1, measures 41–60 (peak at measure 58); the Mazurka in C Minor, Opus 30 No. 1, measures 16–36 (peak at measure 36); the Mazurka in B/F♯ Minor, Opus 30 No. 2, measures 16–32 (peak at measure 31); the Mazurka in D Major, Opus 33 No. 2, measures 49–64 (peak at measure 60); the Mazurka in Ab Major, Opus 50 No. 2, measures 8–28 (peak at measure 26); the Mazurka in Ab Major, Opus 59 No. 2, measures 45–60 (peak at measure 60); the Mazurka in F Minor, Opus 63 No. 2 measures 17–41 (peak at measure 34); the Mazurka in G Minor, Opus 67 No. 2, measures 1–16 (peak at measure 14), and measures 17–32 (peak at measure 32).

EXAMPLE 4.3. Chopin, Waltz in Ab, Opus 34 No. 1, measures 80–96.

while the dynamic curve occurs in midlevel segments, no such tendency was found at higher or lower levels. This suggests that dynamic curve processes, thought by some (e.g., Agawu 1982) to characterize nineteenth-century music generally and at many segmental levels, are confined in some repertories mainly to a single level. While at this medial level the unfolding of a dynamic curve may be an important determinant of continuity, at other levels of segmentation, and in the piece as a whole, overall intensity curves may not play an important structural function.[9]

MELODIC RELATIONSHIPS

A distinctive treatment of peaks in the Chopin repertory is also exhibited by melodic organization. Peaks are emphasized and intensified by both intervallic and tonal-functional melodic relationships. As in Haydn, they are also marked by pitch-register singularity.

Intervals (Tables 4.6, 4.7). Strongly separating them from the preceding line, relatively large upward skips emphasize a majority of peaks in the Chopin sample. The preponderance of such approaches to peaks is evident in the different interval distributions for peaks and controls ($\chi^2 = 48.0, p < .0001$; compare columns I and V, Table 4.6). While a majority (59.5%) of the 200 intervals examined in the control group are conjunct (major or minor seconds), peaks are preceded by conjunct intervals in only a small minority (17.5%) of the examined cases ($p < .001$). Moreover, wide leaps (larger than a perfect fifth), which constitute only 11 percent of the intervals in the control group, are far more frequent (41.3%) in approaches to peaks ($p < .001$). Sixths ($p < .001$) and fourths ($p < .05$) are particularly characteristic,[10] as are skips larger than an octave; the latter, completely absent in the control group—and thus probably a rarity in the repertory as a whole—appear significantly more frequently ($p < .05$) in approaches to peaks (see, e.g., Example 2.8).

What makes this usage remarkable is that it deviates significantly from a widely held, possibly universal preference, for small, conjunct intervals.[11] By catching the listener's attention, such deviation probably emphasizes the effect of the highpoint. For instance, this may be the effect of the frequent use of intervals beyond the octave in approaches to peaks: because such intervals appear rarely in most musical repertories, their use marks the peak for consciousness.

The distribution of intervals following peaks (Table 4.6, column II) is not very

9. In the Chopin repertory, the scarcity of overall dynamic curves is probably due to Chopin's tendency to construct dances out of closed, distinct sections (often in ternary form).

10. For illustrations of approaches by fourths see the Waltz in E♭ Major, Opus 18, measure 27; the Waltz in A♭ Major, Opus 42, measure 150, and the Mazurka in G Major, Opus 50 No. 1, measure 4. Approaches by sixths may be illustrated by the Waltz in D♭ Major, Opus 64 No. 1 measures 32, 50, and by the Mazurka in B♭ Major, Opus 7 No. 1, measure 8.

11. Though skips upward are generally more common than downwards (Vos and Troost, 1989) conjunct intervals were universally found to be the most common in both directions.

TABLE 4.6. Intervals

| | I | | II | | III | | IV | | V | |
	Intervals preceding peaks (n=97)		Intervals following peaks (n=88)		Intervals preceding controls (n=100)		Intervals following controls (n=100)		Interval distribution— controls* (n=200)	
	%	n	%	n	%	n	%	n	%	n
Seconds	17.5	(17)	60.2	(53)	61	(61)	59	(59)	60	(120)
Thirds	17.5	(17)	6.8	(6)	23	(23)	15	(15)	19	(38)
Perfect fourth	20.6	(20)	9.1	(8)	9	(9)	8	(8)	8.5	(17)
Tritone	2.1	(2)	0	(0)	0	(0)	2	(2)	1	(2)
Perfect fifth	1	(1)	4.5	(4)	0	(0)	2	(2)	1	(2)
Augmented fifth	0	(0)	0	(0)	0	(0)	1	(1)	.5	(1)
Sixths	14.5	(14)	2.3	(2)	2	(2)	7	(7)	4.5	(9)
Sevenths	6.2	(6)	2.3	(2)	1	(1)	1	(1)	1	(2)
Octave	11.3	(11)	8	(7)	4	(4)	5	(5)	4.5	(9)
>8va	9.3	(9)	6.8	(6)	0	(0)	0	(0)	0	(0)
Disjunct intervals (>2nds)	82.5	(80)	39.8	(35)	39	(39)	41	(41)	40.5	(81)
>Perfect fifth	41.3	(40)	19.4	(17)	7	(7)	15	(15)	11	(22)

*Column V = Column III + Column IV

different from that of the control group ($p > .05$). In particular, conjunct intervals are nearly as frequent for peaks as for controls, and the frequency of disjunct intervals following peaks is significantly lower ($p < .001$) than their frequency in approaches to peaks. However, a tendency to use extremely large skips can be observed here as well: intervals of an octave or more separate 14.8 percent of the peaks from the following notes, while such intervals constitute only 5 percent of the controls ($p < .01$).[12]

A peak approached and left by large intervals is isolated from its surroundings and thus strongly emphasized. Sometimes (as in the Mazurka in A Minor, Opus 7 No. 2, measures 20–25), isolation highlights a polyphonic configuration within a single line. In other cases registral isolation enhances the sense of large-scale melodic continuity (as Oster 1961 and others have noted). Such is the case in Example 4.4a, where registral isolation highlights the incomplete peak progression E^6–$D\sharp^6$–$C\sharp^6$ (measures 173–175), and thus emphasizes its delayed resolution to B^5 (measure 193; see also the analysis in Example 4.4b).

A particular type of melodic continuity may be generated by an isolated peak

12. The use of large skips (> perfect fifth) in descents from peaks is significantly more frequent in the mazurkas ($p < .05$). See Eitan 1991, app. 7.

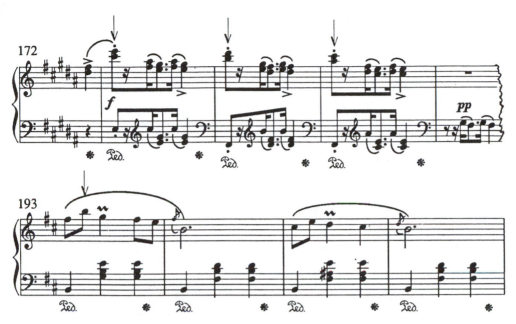

EXAMPLE 4.4A. Chopin, Mazurka in B Minor, Opus 33 No. 4, measures 173–180, 193–196.

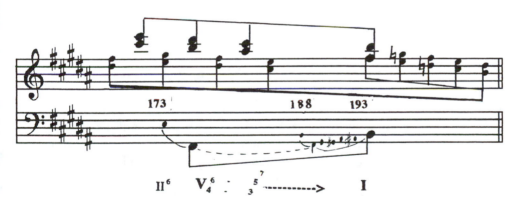

EXAMPLE 4.4B. Registral continuity in Example 4.4a.

in an unaccented metric position. In such cases, the discrepancy between the peak's melodic emphasis and its weak metric position creates a "potential structural tone" — a note "whose melodic prominence is not matched by its structural importance." (Meyer 1973: 196). Such tones strongly imply a realization of their structural potential. Realization may occur when "the same pitch subsequently occurs as an accented structural tone," or "when a subsequent note understood as part of the pattern is an accented structural tone" (ibid.).

The Chopin sample—in particular the waltzes—provides examples of potential structural tones and their subsequent realization. The Waltz in A♭ Major, Opus 42, exhibits a particularly interesting and whimsical instance, in which realization is de-layed until the very end of the piece (Example 4.5). The high-register tonic-chord notes Ab^6 and C^7 are repeatedly emphasized by their appearance as intervallically isolated peaks (in measures 42, 46, 50, 54, and in later repetitions of the same phrase). Yet these notes consistently appear in a metrically weak (third-beat) position until the end of the piece. Only in the last cadence, where they appear as the metrically accented and dynamically emphasized top notes of the terminal tonic (measure 283), are these potential structural tones realized.

Example 4.5 is not the only case in which Chopin uses this strategy in the waltzes and the mazurkas. However, (particularly in the mazurkas), there are cases in which isolated peaks—even ones that occur in a metrically weak position—are not "implicative." In such cases, rather than using peaks to create implicative relation-ships or to enhance long-range connections, Chopin leaves them as unique points of registral accent, strongly marked because they are not part of registral continuity. The peak in measure 44 of Example 2.4 (p. 23) illustrates such registral accent.[13]

To examine whether the preference for larger intervals in approaches to peaks is a manifestation of a general tendency to use large intervals more frequently in ascents, I compared the distribution of ascending intervals (Table 4.7, columns I and II), and descending intervals (columns III and IV) in the peaks and controls. The table shows that the high frequency of disjunct approaches to peaks is not merely a manifestation of ascent. The distribution of ascending intervals at peaks and controls is very dif-ferent ($\chi^2 = 23.92$, $p < .001$; compare columns I and II). While the controls exhibit a significant tendency ($z = 3.02$, $p < .01$) to use disjunct intervals in ascent (column II) more frequently than in descent (column IV), this tendency is considerably more pro-nounced around peaks ($z = 10.16$, $p < .000001$), primarily because disjunct ascents are significantly more frequent for the peaks. In particular, large ascending leaps (more than a perfect fifth), especially sixths and intervals larger than an octave, are considerably more common at peaks ($p < .001$). Table 4.7 also confirms the tendency to leave peaks by large leaps, as it shows that large descending leaps are significantly ($p < .05$) more common at peaks than at controls (columns III and IV).

Melodic emphasis (Table 4.8). Peaks and controls are very different in melodic emphasis as well ($\chi^2 = 27.35$, $p < .00005$, for earlier neighbors; $\chi^2 = 12.96$, $p < .005$, for later neighbors). In most cases, peaks are melodically emphasized relative to *both* their neighbors ($p < .001$, when H0: P(plus) = P(minus)). In other words, intervals approaching melodic peaks are usually larger than those approaching their earlier and later neighbors.

An examination of intervals and of melodic emphasis presents a clear melodic profile of peaks in the examined Chopin repertory: there is an increase in interval size toward the peak, and a decrease after it. The melodic peak is thus characteris-tically also the point of greatest pitch change, and thus a peak of melodic intensity.

---

13. For other examples, see the Mazurka in Bb Major, Opus 17 No. 1 (measure 58), and the Mazurka in B Major, Opus 41 No. 2 (measure 54).

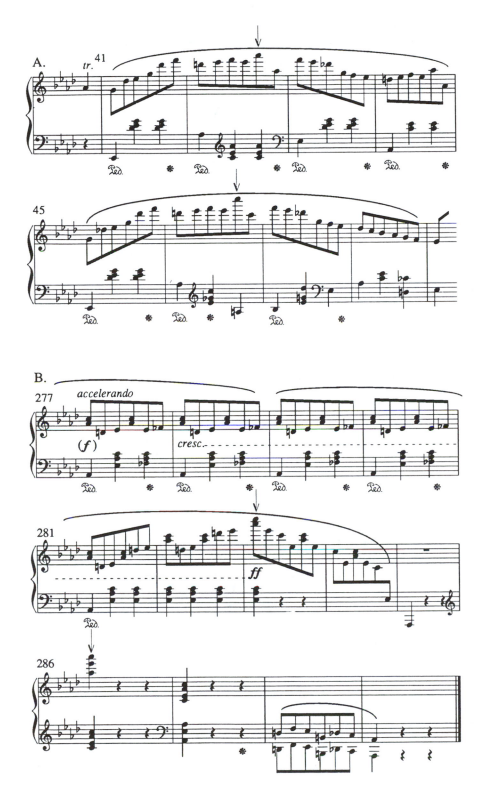

EXAMPLE 4.5. Chopin, Waltz in A♭, Opus 42, measures 40–49, 277–289.

TABLE 4.7. Ascending and descending intervals

Intervals	I Peaks— ascending (n=97)		II Controls— ascending (n=78)		III Peaks— descending (n=88)		IV Controls— descending (n=122)	
	%	n	%	n	%	n	%	n
Seconds	17.5	(17)	48.7	(38)	60.2	(53)	69.7	(85)
Thirds	17.5	(17)	23.1	(18)	6.8	(6)	15.6	(19)
Perfect fourth	20.6	(20)	10.3	(8)	9.1	(8)	5.7	(7)
Perfect fifth	1	(1)	1.3	(1)	4 .5	(4)	.8	(1)
Diminished fifth	2.1	(2)	1.3	(1)	0	(0)	.8	(1)
Sixths	14.5	(14)	6.4	(5)	2.3	(2)	4.1	(5)
Sevenths	6.2	(6)	2.5	(2)	2.3	(2)	0	(0)
Octave	11.3	(11)	6.4	(5)	8	(7)	3.3	(4)
>Octave	9.3	(9)	0	(0)	6.8	(6)	0	(0)
Disjunct intervals (>2nds)	82.5	(80)	51.3	(40)	39.8	(35)	30.3	(37)
>Perfect fifth	43.3	(42)	16.7	(13)	19.4	(17)	7.4	(9)

TABLE 4.8. Melodic emphasis

	Peaks		Controls	
	%	n	%	n
RELATION WITH EARLIER NEIGHBOR				
+	70.8	(68)	34	(34)
=	9.4	(9)	28	(28)
−	19.8	(19)	38	(38)
Total n		96		100
RELATION WITH LATER NEIGHBOR				
+	60.2	(53)	34	(34)
=	14.8	(13)	24	(24)
−	25	(22)	42	(42)
Total n		88		100

TABLE 4.9: Scale degrees

	Relation with local tonic				Relation with main tonic			
	Peaks (n=97)		Controls (n=100)		Peaks (n=97)		Controls (n=100)	
	%	n	%	n	%	n	%	n
$\hat{1}$	24.7	(24)	18	(18)	22.7	(22)	15	(15)
$\hat{2}$	8.2	(8)	6	(6)	7.2	(7)	10	(10)
$\hat{3}$	21.6	(21)	18	(18)	22.7	(22)	14	(14)
$\hat{4}$	6.2	(6)	10	(10)	4.1	(4)	14	(14)
$\hat{5}$	18.6	(18)	24	(24)	17.5	(17)	19	(19)
$\hat{6}$	18.6	(18)	14	(14)	18.6	(18)	14	(14)
$\hat{7}$	2.1	(2)	10	(10)	7.2	(7)	14	(14)
Stable ($\hat{1}, \hat{3}, \hat{5}$)	65	(63)	60	(60)	62.9	(61)	49	(49)
Unstable ($\hat{2}, \hat{4}, \hat{6}, \hat{7}$)	35	(34)	40	(40)	37.1	(36)	51	(51)

By serving as culmination points in this respect, the capacity of peaks to function as affective and emphatic highpoints is strongly enhanced.

The intervallic configuration associated with melodic peaks often creates what has been called the gap-fill structure, a pattern strongly associated with increasing and decreasing tension (Meyer 1973: 145–157). The large leap (or series of leaps) that approaches the peak creates the melodic gap and a tension-inducing implication for its fill, while the conjunct descent from the peak realizes this implication, thus relieving tension. A comparison of the intervals preceding peaks with these following them (Table 4.6 and Table 4.8), as well as an examination of individual examples (e.g., Examples 2.8, 4.1, 4.10) indicate that this tensional gesture is strongly associated with melodic peaks.

Melodic scale degree (Table 4.9). The scale degree of the examined notes was related both to the local tonality and to the main tonality of the piece. In terms of local tonalities, stable degrees ($\hat{1}, \hat{3}, \hat{5}$) are more frequent than unstable ones (with the exception of $\hat{6}$) in both peaks and controls. Though in the peaks the frequency of stable degrees (and of the tonic note in particular) is slightly higher than in the controls, differences between the two groups are small and statistically insignificant ($p > .9$).

However, when scale degree is examined in terms of the principal tonality of each piece, the results are quite different. The controls exhibit a nearly random distribution of scale degrees. The peaks, however, exhibit a significantly different distribution ($p < .05$), and manifest a clear preference for members of the principal tonic triad. The stable degrees of a piece's principal key are, then, frequently employed at its peaks, even when the principal tonality is not apparent on the surface. This suggests that positioning notes of the principal triad at peaks may serve to maintain the reign of the tonic despite surface modulations and, in so doing, reminds the listener that the change of key is temporary.

The Mazurka in G minor, Opus 24 No. 1 (Example 4.6) provides a clear example of this function of melodic peaks. This short piece contains two abrupt key shifts: to the relative major, B♭ (measure 17), and to the subdmediant, E♭ (measure 33). These tonal changes, accompanied by equally abrupt changes in rhythmic and melodic character, seem to threaten the piece's cohesiveness. The use of melodic peaks (together with the overall bass progression) serves to compensate for these abrupt changes. Each of the piece's eight-measure phrases reaches the same peak: the tonic note, G^5 (measures 4, 12, 18, 26, 36, 44, 52, 60, 64). This repeated peak (stressed whenever it appears within a nontonic key area) functions as a subtle reminder of the primacy of the tonic G throughout the piece. At the same time, it serves as an implied upper-voice drone, thus creating a clear, readily perceptible pitch connection between tonally and thematically diverse phrases. The emphatic potential of peaks is thus used as an important structural factor, enhancing long-range continuity and coherence.

Repeated pitches (Table 4.10). My hypothesis that peaks are frequently emphasized by pitch repetition was not confirmed. The opposite is true in the Chopin sample: repeated pitches are significantly less frequent at peaks than at controls ($z = 1.963$, $p < .05$). Rather than emphasizing melodic peaks by repetition, Chopin often uses the opposite strategy: where melodic material comprises mainly repeated-note figures, he differentiates and dramatizes the melodic peak by avoiding its repetition. Cases in point are the Waltz in G♭ Major, Opus 70 No. 1, mm 17–40 (note the peaks at measures 21, 28, and their surroundings) and the Mazurka in F♯ Minor, Opus 6 No. 1, measure 56 (measure 88 in the Fontana version).

Pitch-register singularity (Table 4.11). In the Chopin repertory, pitches featured at melodic peaks are frequently unique within their segment, and in many cases within the entire piece. At the phrase and period levels, the tendency to avoid repetition of melodic peaks nearly achieves the status of a rule. A vast majority of peak pitches appear only once within their period ($z = 8.93$, $p < .0001$). The few exceptions occur when an entire figure is repeated immediately. At a higher level, a quarter of the examined peaks—a significantly large portion—do not recur within the entire piece, except in a context of a repetition or return of the original period; in contrast, all control notes were repeated at the piece level ($z = 7.72$, $p < .0001$).

Peak pitches that appear once within the entire piece sometimes serve as a climax, the structural highpoint of an entire piece. In such cases (e.g., the Mazurka in B Major, Opus 41 No. 2, measure 54),[14] the introduction of a "fresh" pitch emphasizes the piece's climactic point. More often, however, unique peak pitches, appearing either immediately before or at the very end of a piece or large section, serve as a sign: they mark a point of closure or herald its approach. The unprepared introduction

14. Note that in this case not only a single pitch but an entirely new registral zone is introduced.

EXAMPLE 4.6. Chopin, Mazurka in G Minor, Opus 24 No. 1.

EXAMPLE 4.6. Continued.

EXAMPLE 4.6. Continued.

TABLE 4.10. Repeated pitches

	Peaks (n=97)		Controls (n=100)	
	%	n	%	n
Repeated	9.3	(9)	19	(19)
Not repeated	90.7	(88)	81	(81)

TABLE 4.11. Pitch-register singularity

	Peaks (n=97)		Controls (n=100)	
	%	n	%	n
In period	80.5	(78)	18	(18)
In piece	8.2	(8)	0	(0)
In piece (excluding phrase repetitions)	24.7	(24)	0	(0)

of a new register often acts in such cases as a little shock, a surprising and sometimes humorous exclamation point (see, e.g., Waltz in F Major, Opus 34 No. 3, measure 168; Waltz in D♭ Major, Opus 64 No. 1, measure 120).

HARMONY

The peaks differ from the controls in two of the three aspects of harmony investigated. Peaks exhibit a significantly different distribution both of chord morphologies and of soprano positions, but they are not significantly related to specific harmonic degrees.

Harmonic degree (Table 4.12). The comparison of peaks and controls reveals a slight tendency to underline peaks with tonic (I) degrees, while dominant (V) degrees appear relatively infrequently at peaks. These tendencies are not statistically significant, however ($p > .1$), and it seems that peaks in the Chopin repertory are not significantly related to any specific harmonic function.

Chord structure (Table 4.13). The distribution of chord structures at peaks is significantly different from that of controls ($p < .01$). Two specific differences between the groups emerge. First, peaks are more frequently associated with verticalities created by appoggiaturas, suspensions, and other dissonant voice-leading devices (Table 4.13, row f). Examples 2.1, 4.2, and 4.10 are among many instances of this association.[15] Correspondingly, the association of peaks with second-inversion triads —

15. For additional examples see measure 28 of the Waltz in G♭ Major, Opus 70 No. 1, measure 33 of the Mazurka in A Minor, Opus 41 No. 1, and measure 4 of the Mazurka in G Major, Opus 50 No. 1.

TABLE 4.12. Harmonic degrees

Degree	Peaks (n=98)		Controls (n=99)	
	%	n	%	n
I	47.9	(46)	37.4	(37)
V (Including cadential $^6_4$ chords)	30.2	(29)	38.9	(39)
All other degrees	22.5	(22)	23.7	(23)

TABLE 4.13. Chord structure

	Peaks (n=96)		Controls (n=99)	
	%	n	%	n
a. Major or minor triads, $^5_3$ or $^6_3$	40.6	(39)	35.3	(35)
b. Major or minor $^6_4$ triads	8.3	(8)	3	(3)
c. Diminished or augmented triads	3.1	(3)	2	(2)
d. Dominant seventh chords	12.6	(12)	28.3	(28)
e. Other seventh chords	1	(1)	6.1	(6)
f. All other verticalities [17]	34.4	(33)	25.3	(25)
d+e	13.6	(13)	34.4	(34)
b+f	42.7	(41)	28.3	(28)

chords that also function as dissonant contrapuntal configurations—is relatively frequent as well (note the b and b + f rows; for the latter, $p < .05$ when H0: P (peaks) = P (control)). The Mazurkas in A minor, Opus 59 No. 1 (measure 9) and Opus 68 No. 2 (measure 31); the Waltz in C♯ Minor, Opus 64 No. 2 (measure 13); and the Waltz in E♭ Major, KK IVb No. 10 (measure 14) illustrate the use of second-inversion triads at peaks.[16] Second, peaks are rarely associated with seventh chords, the dominant seventh chord in particular: the frequency of the association of peaks with seventh chords is considerably lower than that of the controls ($p < .01$; see rows d, e, and the combined d + e category in Table 4.13).

Soprano position (Table 4.14). The soprano positions of peaks and controls are significantly different ($p < .01$). In accord with results for chord structure, peaks function more frequently as nonharmonic tones ($p < .05$), particularly as ninths or thir-

16. These results are the opposite of those in the Haydn sample, in which second-inversion triads were avoided at peaks. Haydn, as observed, mostly presents the top notes of such chords as passing notes, thus preventing these sensitive and tensional configurations from being further emphasized by the upper-line contour. In contrast, Chopin often uses voice-leading configurations that result in melodic peaks over second-inversion chords (as well as over other tensional verticalities), and thus emphasize these verticalities contourally.

17. Primarily verticalities including nonharmonic tones.

TABLE 4.14. Soprano positions

	Peaks (n=96)		Controls (n=99)	
	%	n	%	n
CHORDAL TONES	67.7	(65)	78.9	(78)
8 (root)	34.3	(33)	21.2	(21)
3	18.8	(18)	22.2	(22)
5	11.5	(11)	20.2	(20)
7	3.1	(3)	15.1	(15)
NON-HARMONIC TONES	32.3	(31)	20.3	(21)
9	15.6	(15)	9.1	(9)
11 (4)	3.1	(3)	5.1	(5)
13 (6)	13.6	(13)	7.1	(7)

teenths. In contrast, they rarely function as sevenths ($p < .01$). However, peaks also function more frequently than controls as the root of the chord to which they belong ($p < .05$).

Harmonic Tendencies

Two significant and somewhat puzzling tendencies are revealed by this examination of harmonic and tonal features. First, peaks in the Chopin sample are emphasized by two seemingly contradictory means. On the one hand, they are associated with harmonically stable elements, such as stable degrees of the principal key, or a chord's root—its most stable pitch class. On the other hand, peaks are frequently associated with "non-harmonic" tones—transitory, "surface" dissonances. Second, peaks are seldom associated with seventh chords. This tendency is manifested directly by chord structure (Table 4.13) and indirectly by the scarcity of peaks functioning as sevenths in their respective chords (Table 4.14). It is also evident in the relatively low frequency of dominant degrees (which mostly appear as seventh chords).

How can these tendencies be explained? The relative infrequency of seventh chords at peaks might stem from voice-leading considerations. Of the four possible soprano positions of a seventh chord, three create voice-leading problems when the uppermost part is a melodic peak. In octave positions, a descending progression in the upper part is likely to create hidden octaves, as in Example 4.7a (if stationary, the peak is "shared" by two or more chords and not associated with the seventh chord alone). Third positions are problematic in major-minor ("dominant") seventh chords (which constitute the majority of seventh chords in this repertory), where the third is a leading tone, resolved upward (Example 4.7b). Finally, in seventh positions the upper

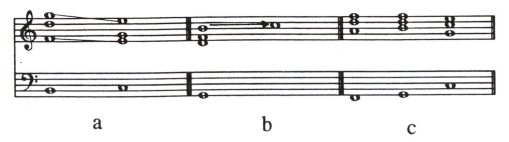

a   b   c

EXAMPLE 4.7. Melodic peaks and the resolution of dominant seventh-chords.

part would often be prepared (even in Chopin's "free" voice leading), and the peak would thus not be associated with the seventh chord alone (Example 4.7c). Though Chopin's "free" counterpoint is capable of getting around (or simply ignoring) problematic voice-leading, these problems provide at least a partial explanation for the scarcity of seventh chords at peaks.

The association of peaks with harmonic features of contrasting import indicates that their emphatic force is employed for diverse structural purposes, not only to create climactic "structural highpoints." Associating peaks with agents of "grammatical" emphasis, such as the tonic note or chord, underlines tonal hierarchy; their association with striking dissonances, agents of "rhetorical" emphasis, highlights points of intensity.[18]

In Example 4.6 (p. 93) a subtle interplay between these two types of emphasis shapes an entire piece. As already noted, the principal tonic note G^5 repeatedly serves in this mazurka as a peak, even when another key is temporarily tonicized. In the stable outer sections of the piece, when the principal key, G minor, is maintained, this peak marks points of closure—cadential points of grammatical emphasis (mm. 4, 12, 52, 60, 64). Accordingly, it is associated with stable harmonic features: the tonic chord, consonance, an octave soprano position. When another key is temporarily established, the same peak pitch marks tense, instable points of local climax—points of rhetorical emphasis (mm. 18, 26, 36, 44), and is related to tensional harmonic features, such as nonharmonic dissonance and unstable harmonic degrees.[19] Even at these points of tonal instability, however, the primary tonic note is maintained as the peak. A locus of rhetorical emphasis, while itself "open" and unstable, is thus associated with tonal stability and closure—with grammatical emphasis.

The tendency for peaks to be associated with either grammatical or rhetorical emphasis may partly explain the scarcity of seventh chords at peaks in this repertory. Seventh chords are hierarchically dependent on the verticalities they resolve to and

18. The distinction between grammatical and rhetorical emphasis is suggested in Chapter 1, pp. 7–8.

19. Note also that the harmonically stable peaks in this piece are metrically accented, while the harmonically instable ones appear on stressed upbeats. Thus, meter supports harmony in differentiating a "grammatical" usage of peaks from a "rhetorical" one.

TABLE 4.15. Dynamic emphases

	Peaks (n=97)		Controls (n=100)	
	%	n	%	n
Processive (end of *crescendo*)	18 .6	(18)	3	(3)
Local (accent, *Sfz*)	20.6	(20)	11	(11)

thus are deemphasized grammatically; but most create relatively mild dissonance (as compared, for instance, to many nonharmonic dissonances frequent at peaks), that are too weak to create a sufficient rhetorical emphasis. Their dissociation from peaks is thus based not on voice-leading grounds alone: it indicates again, in a negative way, the strong association of the melodic peak with emphatic features.[20]

DYNAMICS

Dynamic emphasis (Table 4.15). Melodic peaks in the Chopin sample are significantly associated with processive dynamic emphases ($z = 3.52$, $p < .001$) but not with local ones ($z = 1.85$, $p > .05$); that is, they are often situated at the end of *crescendi*, but are not significantly associated with local stresses, such as *sforzandi*. (though, of course, many cases of such association exist, for instance in Example 4.6).

Most of the melodic peaks marked by processive dynamic emphasis are preceded by rather direct ascents, which closely parallel the *crescendi*. These range from short, steep rises to the peak, as in Example 4.8,[21] to long, gradual ascents, paralleled by a "*poco a poco crescendo*," such as Example 4.9.

Such direct parallelisms create a clear and "natural" correspondence between two types of heightening intensity, an ascent in pitch and increasing dynamics. This intensification of melodic peaks is often enhanced by concurrent intensifying harmonic progressions. In many cases, moreover, notated *crescendi* are reserved mainly or solely to ascents toward prominent melodic peaks, thus indicating to the performer that these are important points, demanding emphasis.

20. Leonard B. Meyer has suggested (personal communication) an alternative explanation to the scarcity of dominant seventh chords at peaks. Meyer proposes that because peaks often open a melodic gap that may call for a gradual and rather lengthy fill, their placement on top of dominant seventh chords, which imply an immediate resolution to the tonic, may be problematic. In such cases, the instant harmonic resolution would not properly resolve the gap-induced melodic tension. Meyer also notes that the familiarity of the dominant-seventh sonority may detract from the markedness of the peak—another reason to avoid this configuration at such points.

21. For similar gestures see, e.g., the Waltz in Eb Major, Opus 18, measure 27; The Waltz in Gb Major, Opus 70 No. 1 (Fontana version), measures 17–18; and the Mazurka in C Major, Opus 24 No. 2, measures 25–26.

EXAMPLE 4.8. Chopin, Waltz in A♭, Opus 34 No. 1, measures
91–92.

EXAMPLE 4.9. Chopin, Mazurka in B (F♯) Minor, Opus 30 No. 2, measures 24–32.

PARAMETRIC INTERACTION

Combined parametric emphasis (Table 4.16). This summarizing category further indicates a strong inclination in the Chopin repertory to present peaks emphatically, combining durational, metric, and intervallic procedures. There is a highly significant difference ($\chi^2 = 24.47$, $p < .001$) between peaks and controls in the distribution of the four degrees of combined emphasis. Particularly, the high emphasis category is far more frequent at peaks, while the medium-low and low emphasis categories are considerably less frequent.

Example 4.10 demonstrates one of many cases in which durational, metric, and intervallic emphases (as well as other sources of salience) conspire to create a forceful highpoint (measure 13). The force of an extremely large upward leap is enhanced by

TABLE 4.16. Combined parametric emphasis

	Peaks (n=97)		Controls (n=100)	
	%	n	%	n
High (4–6)	37.1	(36)	16	(16)
Medium-high (1–3)	33	(32)	24	(24)
Medium-low (−2–0)	25.8	(25)	47	(47)
Low (−6−−3)	4.1	(4)	13	(13)

a strong metric accent (supported by the left-hand pattern) and agogic emphasis. A dynamic emphasis and a sharp, unprepared dissonance (a ninth) further heighten this point of stress and tension. The C^6 peak is also marked as the completion of a triadic melodic process that moves from Eb^5 (measure 9) through Ab^5 (measure 11) to C^6 (measure 13), a pattern prefigured by a similar triadic structure in the opening phrase (C^5, measure 1–F^5, measure 3–Ab^5, measure 6).[22]

Interparametric congruence (Tables 4.17–4.19). An investigation of interparametric congruence reveals the presence of normative tendencies toward congruence between parametric emphases—tendencies that connect metric accent with two other kinds of emphasis, durational and melodic. These normative tendencies, however, are either absent or considerably weakened in the case of melodic peaks.

The tendency toward congruence between metric and durational emphases is particularly strong. In the control group, such congruence is far more frequent than that expected from a random interaction between these parameters (EFr).[23] Correspondingly, the actual frequency of metric-durational noncongruences is considerably lower than its EFr ($\chi^2 = 34.48$, $p < .001$). These results are not surprising, because periodic durational accents probably play an important role in shaping the perception of metric structure.

A significant tendency toward congruence ($p < .01$) also exists between metric and melodic emphases (Table 4.18). As with meter and duration, the actual frequency of metric-melodic congruence in the control group is considerably above EFr, while the opposite is true for noncongruences between these parameters.

22. Note that while the two triadic patterns are analogous melodically, they are substantially different harmonically. The peak of the opening pattern (m. 6) is a harmonically stable component of the tonic chord, while the melodically analogous peak (C, m. 13) is an instable appoggiatura, a "nonharmonic" tone. Thus, while the opening triadic pattern may be interpreted as a "true" voice-leading pattern, an arppeggiation prolonging the initial F minor tonic harmony, its counterpart cannot be interpreted analogously as a prolongation of the mediant (III). While its beginning (mm. 9–11) implies such an analogy, this implication is strongly denied at the ensuing peak. While realizing a melodic implication, the peak simultaneously denies a harmonic one. This clash of melody and harmony further contributes to its status as a highpoint of tension.

23. See the convergence of the plus column with the plus row and of the minus column with the minus row in the control portion of Table 4.17.

EXAMPLE 4.10. Chopin, Waltz in F Minor, Opus 70, No. 2, measures 1–20.

TABLE 4.17. Congruence between durational and metric emphases

Meter	Duration						
	Peaks			Controls			
	+	−		+	−		
+	71 (66)	14 (19)	85	41 (27)	9 (23)	50
−	17 (22)	12 (7)	29	8 (22)	34 (20)	42
	88	26	114	49	43	92

TABLE 4.18. Congruence between metric and melodic emphases

Meter	Melody						
	Peaks			Controls			
	+	−		+	−		
+	72 (72)	26 (26)	98	41 (33)	31 (39)	72
−	35 (35)	12 (12)	47	20 (28)	42 (34)	62
	107	38	145	61	73	134

TABLE 4.19. Congruence between durational and melodic emphases

Duration	Melody						
	Peaks			Controls			
	+	−		+	−		
+	53 (55)	24 (22)	77	20 (18)	20 (22)	40
−	19 (17)	5 (7)	24	12 (14)	19 (17)	31
	72	29	101	32	39	71

In contrast, durational and melodic emphases show no inclination toward congruence or noncongruence ($p > .3$; see Table 4.19). Though congruence between durational and melodic emphases is frequent in the control group, this high frequency reflects EFr closely and thus has limited importance.

The deviations from the EFrs, found in the controls, are either diminished or altogether absent in the peaks. This indicates that general tendencies toward interparametric congruence are absent or considerably weaken at peaks. Regarding metric-durational congruence (Table 4.17), deviations from EFr in the peaks are considerably smaller than in the controls ($\chi^2 = 5.22$, $p < .05$ for peaks; $\chi^2 = 34.48$, $p < .001$ for controls). With regard to metric-melodic congruence, actual frequencies in the peaks are practically identical with the EFr ($p > .9$; Table 4.18): the tendency toward congruence between these two parameters, observed in the control group, is eliminated at melodic peaks.[24]

How do these findings relate to the our principal hypotheses? First, in Chopin melodic peaks are indeed significantly different in interparametric congruence from other points along the melodic curve. Second, deviation from interparametric relations that are near-normative in the repertory enhances the tensional character of peaks, especially when such deviations create conflicts between emphases, thereby introducing an uncertainty that enhances tension. Some of the affective force of peaks may, then, be traced to deviations from such stylistic norms.

CONCLUSION

Results in the Chopin sample, in contrast to those in Haydn, confirm the initial hypotheses of this study: the comparison of peaks and controls presents a preference for the use of specific metric, durational, intervallic, and functional relations at peaks. Moreover, virtually all these relations enhance emphasis, and many are traditionally related to the heightening of tension.

Among other things, the Chopin results show that peaks are often distinguished by both metric and durational emphasis, often marked melodically by wide intervallic approaches and by pitch-register singularity, and often highlighted by concurrent dynamic culmination. Important (though not as immediately apparent) emphasis is often also created through the association of peaks with the principal tonic note. The presence of sharp dissonances, created by appoggiaturas and other "nonharmonic" tones, also enhances the emphasis of peaks.

It is widely acknowledged that several of these phenomena also enhance tension and strong affect, for example, the gap-creating use of wide leaps and the frequent use of peaks as appoggiaturas. A tendency toward noncongruence between emphases in different parameters (such as metric and agogic emphases) further marks melodic peaks as points of heightened tension.

When compared to the Haydn results, the Chopin findings are enlightening. While the emphatic and tensional potential of melodic peaks is frequently undermined in Haydn, in Chopin it is repeatedly enhanced and highlighted in diverse ways. Contour peaks in Chopin are thus salient points in the musical discourse and often points of utmost tension. This use of peaks has more than a local significance: their salience makes them important structural and expressive devices. Thus, peaks frequently function in the Chopin repertory as the culmination points of midlevel dynamic curves (a

---

24. Note that the investigation of interparametric congruence does not refer to the frequencies of congruent relationships per se, but to the relations between these actual frequencies and the frequencies expected from a random interaction of emphases in the two parameter concerned, given the results in each parameter. See Chapter 2, pp. 28–29.

fact indicated by their tendency to appear near the end of midlevel segments), playing a crucial role in process that became increasingly important in nineteenth-century music (Agawu 1982; Meyer 1989, pt. 3). In addition, the salience of melodic peaks enables them to clarify tonal processes, as in cases where the retention of a tonic peak strengthens the principal tonality amid surface modulations.

The findings suggest that contour peaks, and by implication the psychologically natural dimension of contour, are important in shaping structure and expression in the Chopin repertory. The limited scope of the samples does not allow generalizations beyond the specific composers surveyed. Yet Chopin's increased reliance on melodic shape may well embody an important characteristic of nineteenth-century Romanticism. This dependence on a "natural" means of expression is in line with a prominent theme in nineteenth-century ideology and may have been, for more than one reason, a compositional necessity for Romantic composers. The superiority of natural constraints in art (and the corresponding slighting of learned convention) has been an important tenet of nineteenth-century Romantic ideology. As Rosen and Zerner (1979: 27) comment, Romantic artists aimed at "the achievement of 'immediacy' " through "forms of expression directly understandable without convention and without previous knowledge of tradition." Specifically, the direct, natural expression of emotion was highly valued. Perhaps one reason music was hailed as the most suitable instrument for such purposes is that the human emotional world was often supposed to "present [itself] directly to the ear through the *tone of voice*" (Wagner [1850] 1965: 141), namely through voice (and particularly speech) intonation. With the "tone of voice" considered a paradigm of natural emotive expression, and the unmediated expression of natural affect hailed as the highest artistic purpose, it is scarcely surprising that melodic contour—the "tone" of the musical "voice"—became a prime expressive and structural resource.

The increased importance of contour (and of other "secondary" dimensions, such as dynamics) may have served both compositional and social purposes. The increased complexity of tonal syntax in the nineteenth century—for instance, the more extensive use of chromaticism, the broadening of the range of modulation, and the freer voice leading—might have necessitated an increased reliance on nonsyntactical dimensions such as contour to clarify structure.[25] In addition, the growing significance of nonsyntactical, secondary parameters may be related to a decline in audience sophistication, from a musically educated, aristocratic audience to a wider, yet less knowledgeable, middle-class public. Because much of this new audience was less aware of the conventional nuances of tonal syntax, conventional syntax had to be supported by more natural, nonsyntactical gestures.[26] Thus, the increased reliance on melodic shape and other "natural" dimensions might have been a result of ideology (unconsciously applied), as well as a solution to a compositional problem and an outcome of changes in the social context of music.

25. Such reliance is exemplified, with regard to Mahler, in Hopkins 1990.
26. A similar observation was made by Meyer 1989: 208–11.

CHAPTER 5

Peaks in Berg: Romantic Gesture in a New Context

Melodic peaks in four of Berg's compositions were examined in this study: the *Four Pieces for Clarinet and Piano*, Opus 5 (1913), the *Lyric Suite* (1926), *Der Wein* (1929), and the first two acts of *Lulu* (1930–35).[1]

Even though I selected only posttonal and serial pieces (as opposed to the early tonal pieces), the examined repertory covers a wide range of genres and styles. To control some of the variables, I analyzed not only the Berg sample as a whole but also vocal and instrumental pieces separately (see Eitan 1991, vol. 2, app. 6). Although these two bodies of music are conspicuously different in both compositional language and precompositional technique (for one thing, both *Der Wein* and *Lulu* are dodecaphonic pieces, while in the two earlier works only two movements of the *Lyric Suite* are), my analysis reveals very few differences between them.[2] Thus, it seems appropriate to view the results as applicable to Berg's posttonal style in general.

Berg's music discussed here contrasts with the repertories analyzed in the preceding chapters in an obvious way: while pitch relationships in the music of both Haydn and Chopin are regulated by tonal syntax, in Berg's music (his many allusions to tonal harmony notwithstanding) pitch relationships are constrained by very different principles. This break in pitch "grammar," however, does not entail a cor-

1. I selected peaks from the clarinet part in the *Four Pieces for Clarinet and Piano* and from the vocal part in *Der Wein*. In the *Lyric Suite* I examined the highest pitch in a section (regardless of instrument), but only if it is included in a phrase designated a primary or secondary voice (Hauptstimme or Nebenstimme). Incidentally, nearly all peaks are part of a Hauptstimme, an indication of their structural significance. In *Lulu* I selected peaks from the principal vocal part in each number. Where no vocal part is clearly dominant, I selected the peak from the highest vocal part.

2. About Berg's stylistic development, see Perle 1985, chapter 1 and Jarman 1979, especially chapters 2 and 3.

responding change in melodic gesture. Rather, in nearly all aspects considered here, Berg's handling of peaks continues and strengthens tendencies observed in Chopin's tonal, Romantic corpus. As in Chopin, peaks in Berg are often points of intense climax, strongly emphasized by duration, meter, temporal location, melodic intervals and dynamics. Further, Berg frequently associates peaks with gestures and strategies prevalent in nineteenth-century music. For instance, he presents series of progressively "stretched" peaks (a series of peaks in which duration, pitch height, and the intervals approaching peaks are progressively increased); he features extended, exaggerated variants of gap-fill gestures; and he uses peaks to create long-range pitch connections, sometimes engendering nested motivic configurations.

Berg, however, does not simply imitate Romantic idioms. Rather, his use of nineteenth-century melodic gestures exaggerates and tilts the original configurations. Further, the presentation of Romantic gestures in an alien syntactic environment often produces strange results, sometimes clashing with the gesture's original ramifications.

Berg's use of old gestures within a new environment calls for discussion and exemplification. Hence, the format of this chapter sometimes deviates from that of chapters 3 and 4. As the preceding chapters, this one presents the statistical results aspects by aspect. However, I often digress in this chapter to discuss gestures and strategies that cannot be directly presented statistically. In particular, following the discussion of durational and metric emphasis, I consider Berg's use of durational stretching; following the presentation of results for melodic intervals I discuss various melodic strategies associated with peaks in this music: gap-fill gestures, intervallic stretching, the "terminal fall" gesture, and the long-range connections among peaks.

DURATIONAL AND METRIC RELATIONSHIPS

Melodic peaks in the Berg repertory are strongly associated with both durational and metric emphases.

Durational emphasis (Table 5.1). The difference in durational emphasis between peaks and controls in the Berg sample is highly significant ($\chi^2 = 33.07$, $p < .001$ for earlier neighbors; $\chi^2 = 30.74$, $p < .001$ for later neighbors). This level is considerably higher than that observed in Chopin or Haydn. Further, a sizable majority of peaks in the sample are longer than *both* neighbors ($z = 5.25$, $p < .001$; see Table 5.1c), while peaks shorter or equal in duration to both neighbors are rare ($z = 2.96$, $p < .005$).

Metric location (Table 5.2). Peaks and controls exhibit a highly significant difference in metric location ($\chi^2 = 18.44$, $p < .001$), considerably higher than that observed in either of the other two repertories. In particular, peaks frequently occur at downbeats ($p < .0001$), and infrequently at offbeat locations ($p < .001$).

Metric emphasis (Table 5.3). Results indicate a tendency to emphasize peaks metrically. This tendency is strong relative to earlier neighbors ($\chi^2 = 11.75$, $p < .01$), and weaker, though discernible, relative to later neighbors ($\chi^2 = 3.69$, $.1 > p > .05$).

TABLE 5.1. Durational emphasis

	Peaks		Controls	
	%	n	%	n
RELATION WITH EARLIER NEIGHBOR				
+	66.7	(56)	23.3	(20)
=	23.8	(20)	46.5	(40)
−	9.5	(8)	30.2	(26)
Total n		84		86
RELATION WITH LATER NEIGHBOR				
	62.7	(47)	21.2	(18)
	20	(15)	56.5	(48)
	17.3	(13)	22.3	(19)
Total n		75		85
SELECTED RELATIONS TO BOTH NEIGHBORS				
	Peaks (n=74)		Controls (n=84)	
+ +	55.4	(41)	15.5	(13)
= =	13.5	(10)	33.3	(28)

TABLE 5.2. Metric location

	Peaks (n=86)		Controls (n=86)	
Location	%	n	%	n
On beats	68.6	(59)	43.6	(37.5)
On 1st beat	32.5	(28)	11	(9.5)
On other beats	36.1	(31)	32.6	(28)
Off-beats	31.4	(27)	56.4	(48.5)

Uses of Metric and Durational Emphasis

The preceding statistics clearly indicate that durational and metrical emphasis of peaks is normative in the Berg repertory. This interaction of contoural, agogic, and metric emphases often plays an important role in both the structural and the expressive domains. Noteworthy is the role of such interactions in shaping thematic gestures and in relating them to each other. For instance, the principal motives of both the first

Table 5.3. Metric emphasis

	Peaks		Controls	
	%	n	%	n
RELATION WITH EARLIER NEIGHBOR				
+	61.2	(52)	34.9	(30)
=	11.8	(10)	20.9	(18)
−	27	(23)	44.2	(38)
Total n		85		86
RELATION WITH LATER NEIGHBOR				
+	49.3	(37)	35.3	(30)
=	24	(18)	25.9	(22)
−	26.7	(20)	38.8	(33)
Total n		75		85

and the fourth movements of the *Lyric Suite*—motives that shape the bulk of those two movements—consist of an urgent thrust upward to sustained, accented peaks, followed by an immediate abatement (Examples 5.1 and 5.2). These statements, like others in the piece, are thus related by gestural similarity, which creates a coherence of a different (yet no less important) kind than that achieved by the intricate dodecaphonic relations and self-quotations prevalent in the piece.

In both of the vocal works examined, peaks endowed with extreme durational emphasis characteristically mark points of major cadential or dramatic significance. This is particularly evident in *Der Wein*. In each of the three songs of the piece (*Die Seele des Weines*, measures 1–87; *Der Wein der Liebenden*, measures 88–172; *Der Wein des Einsamen*, measures 173–216), the vocal line ends with an elongated peak (see Examples 5.3, 5.4, and 5.16, measures 81, 136, and 207 respectively). In the first two songs this peak is the longest and the highest note in the entire melodic line. Moreover, all three peaks highlight climactic points in Baudelaire's text.

Long-lasting, extremely high peaks, marking both an approaching closure and a point of heightened dramatic significance, are also prominent in *Lulu*. The progressively stretched series of peaks in Alwa's and Lulu's parts near the end of Act II (Example 5.8, measures 1134–36 and 1142 in Alwa's part, measures 1139–40 in Lulu's) is a case in point. So is Lulu's cry at the end of Act II, Scene 1, the opera's climactic scene (Example 5.5, measures 647–48). Extremely elongated melodic peaks also mark the dramatic climaxes in this scene: the schoolboy's cry for help, which turns Dr. Schön from a murderer to a murdered man (measures 503–504), and the moment of Schön's death, marked by a sustained melodic apex in the orchestra (measures 605–607).

Durational stretching. Peaks gain distinctive expressive force through the strat-

EXAMPLE 5.1. Berg, *Lyric Suite*, 1st movement, measures 1–4. Copyright 1927, renewed 1954 by Universal Edition, A.G., Vienna.

egy of durational stretching. Stretching "for any parameter of music [involves] an increase in degree relative to some nonsyntactic standard or precedent."[3] With respect to melodic peaks, durational stretching lengthens later peaks in a phrase or section in relation to earlier ones (with which they sometimes share rhythmic or intervallic motives) or to some standard (intra- or extra-opus) of "normal" duration.

A^5, the peak in Example 5.16 (p. 120, measure 81) is durationally stretched in relation to standards such as local context, norms established in the piece as a whole, and extra-opus norms. The duration of peaks in this phrase (E^5 at measure 78, F^5 at measure 80, A^5 at measure 81) gradually increases, culminating in the whole-note A^5 that terminates it, up in the sky ("Zur Himmel"). Further, this peak is the longest-held

---

3. Meyer 1989: 259. For a discussion of stretching and its roles in nineteenth-century music, see pages 259–71.

EXAMPLE 5.2. Berg, *Lyric Suite*, 4th movement, measures 1–4. Copyright 1927, renewed 1954 by
Universal Edition, A.G., Vienna.

vocal note heard since the piece's beginning. Finally, a high-register vocal note held
for approximately five seconds (the tempo is quarter note = 46–52) stretches extra-
opus durational standards, and imparts a quality of physiological strain. Example 5.5
contains an even more straightforward case of durational stretching. Each of the ascending sequential figures that compose this phrase (measures 637–638, 639–641,
641–644) is longer than the preceding one, and a corresponding process involves the
peaks of these figures (G^5, measure 637, A^5, measure 639, B^5, measure 641). The $C\#^6$
peak at measures 647–48 brings this process to its culmination.

In the vocal works, such strategies not only contribute to expressive and structural articulation, but also have specific dramatic and textual connotations. This is
evident in Example 5.5, where the durational stretching intensifies Lulu's repeated
plea to Alwa. Similarly, in Example 5.6 the text consists of several utterances of a

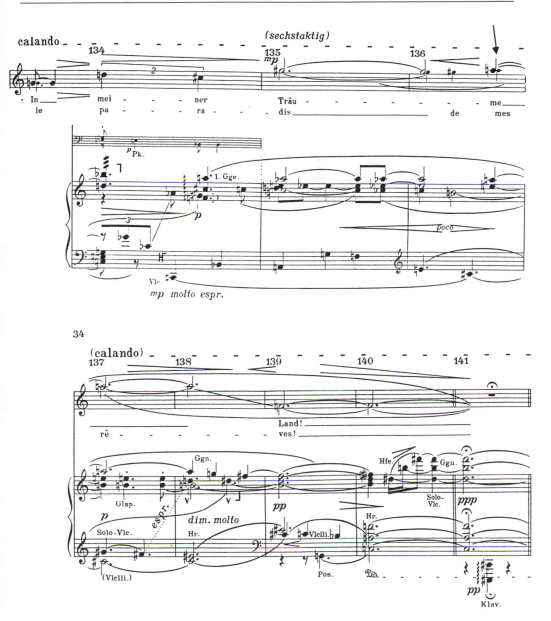

EXAMPLE 5.3. Berg, *Der Wein*: *Der Wein der Liebenden*, measures 134–141. Copyright 1951 by Universal Edition, A.G., Vienna.

single idea, intensified in each utterance ("Er sicht nicht; er sicht mich nicht und sich nicht. Er ist blind, blind, blind . . ."). This intensification is again expressed by the ascending sequence in Lulu's line, culminating with a durationally stretched peak (D^6, measure 557). In Example 5.7 the terminal motive of the phrase clearly relates to the opening one (sharing its contour and its rhythmic patterning) while stretching both its

EXAMPLE 5.4. Berg, *Der Wein*: *Der Wein des Einsamen*, measures 206–210. Copyright 1951 by Universal
Edition, A.G., Vienna.

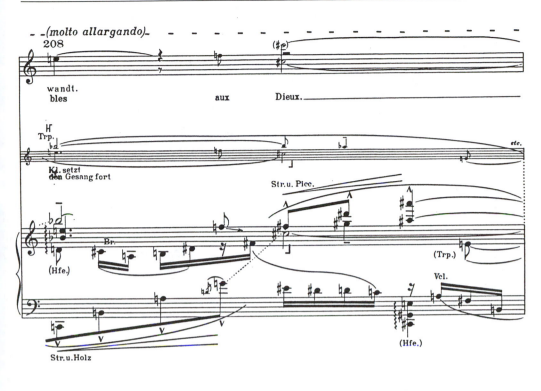

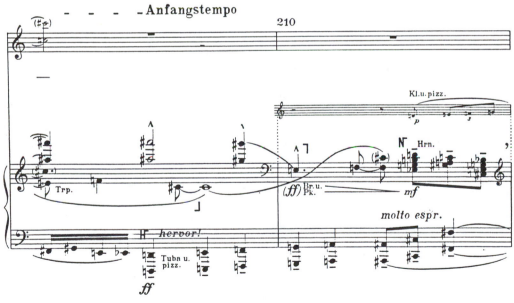

EXAMPLE 5.4. Continued.

EXAMPLE 5.5. Berg, *Lulu*, Act II, Scene 1, measures 637–649. Copyright 1936 by Universal Edition, A.G., Vienna.

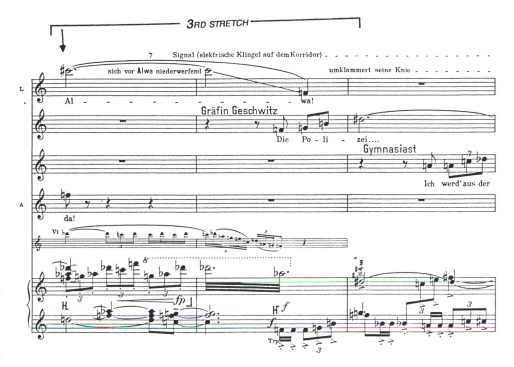

EXAMPLE 5.5. Continued.

intervals and the duration of the peak. Once more, this relation is dramatically relevant: the phrase begins with Lulu's warning to the painter, who tries to seduce her, "my husband would soon be here" (the "standard," unstretched phrase); it continues with the two hearing somebody coming, and culminates with Lulu's cry of relief "thank God" (the stretched motive) as the noises seem to be only the caretaker's. The stretch thus serves as a dramatic purpose (though a low-level one), a culmination and relief of the tension generated by the opening, "standard" motive.

Syncopation (Table 5.4, p. 98). Syncopation is not particularly associated with peaks in the Berg sample ($z = 1.09$, $p > .05$).

Temporal location (Table 5.5). A strong tendency to place peaks at the later parts of segments is exhibited at all the levels investigated in Berg, from short segments (5–10 measures), through large sections (such as entire numbers in *Lulu*, or each of the three songs composing *Der Wein*), to entire movements and pieces. Statistically, this tendency is evident in a significant difference in location between peaks and controls, a difference that is due to the large number of peaks located in the second half, and particularly in the last quarter of segments.[4] Though the late-location tendency

4. At the lower level, a chi-square test demonstrated a significant difference in the temporal distribution of peaks and controls ($\chi^2 = 14.47$, $p < .01$; alternative computation, with H0 assuming even distribution: $\chi^2 = 10.48$, $p < .05$). Specifically, standard-score tests indicate a tendency to position peaks in the later half of segments ($z = 3.69$, $p < .001$), in their last quarter ($z = 2.63$, $p < .01$), and as their

EXAMPLE 5.6. Berg, *Lulu*, Act I, Scene 2, measures 553–557. Copyright 1936 by Universal Edition, A.G., Vienna.

EXAMPLE 5.7. Berg, *Lulu*, Act I, Scene 1, measures 137–141. Copyright 1936 by Universal Edition, A.G., Vienna.

TABLE 5.4. Syncopation

	Peaks (n=86)		Controls (n=86)	
	%	n	%	n
Syncopated	18.6	(16)	12.8	(11)
Not syncopated	83.4	(70)	87.2	(75)

is significant at all levels, it is strongest—as in Chopin—in the mid-level (phrase-group) segmental level ($\chi^2 = 28.14$, $p < .001$). Both middle and high levels show a corresponding tendency to avoid peaks in the segment's opening quarter. In addition, peaks often are terminal notes of low-level segments ($z = 3.83$, $p < .001$).[5]

The appearance of a peak near the end of a segment may serve different functions. A peak may be the culmination point of an intensifying process shaped by an ascending contour, among other techniques. In such a case, the late appearance of the melodic peak is related to a tendency to place climactic areas near the end of a piece or a section. However, a late peak can also be a local sign of impending closure, a sign not necessarily related to the culmination of a long-range process of intensification. These two functions seem to characterize peaks in Chopin and Haydn, respectively. The roles of melodic peaks as points of climax and as conventional signs of closure do not necessarily exclude each other, however, and in the examined Berg sample a melodic peak often serves in both capacities.

The use of late peaks as signs of closure is indicated by cadential patterns such as the "terminal fall" gesture—a huge fall from a peak, prevalent at the end of sections—or by the introduction of "fresh," long-unused pitches at peaks near the end of pieces and large sections (both strategies are discussed below, pp. 103, 129–33). Other strategies reflect the climactic function of late peaks. For instance, late peaks often serve as the culmination of ascending patterns of lesser peaks (frequently in

---

last note ($z = 3.83$, $p < .001$). In mid-level segments, $\chi^2 = 28.14$, $p < .001$ (alternative computation, with H0 assuming even distribution, $\chi^2 = 15.18$, $p < .01$). Standard-score tests demonstrated a significant tendency to place peaks in the last quarter of segments ($z = 4.41$, $p < .001$) and at their second half ($z = 5.26$ $p < .001$), and a tendency to avoid placing them early in the segment ($z = 3.97$, $p < .001$). At the higher level, $\chi^2 = 13.24$ ($p < .01$). Again, standard score tests are significant for the second half ($z = 3.1$, $p < .005$) and for the last ($z = 2.71$, $p < .01$) and first ($z = 2.97$, $p < .01$) quarters.

5. The prevalence of late peaks in the Berg repertory is also indicated in the tone rows in the examined dodecaphonic pieces: the highest note in the original (P) form of most of these rows appears late in the series. In repertories where the twelve-tone series is an abstract set of intervallic relationships (for instance, in Webern's serial pieces), such observation would have been of little importance. However, Berg's rows are often presented as "motives," whose contour is as important as their intervallic construction and is sometimes preserved even at the expense of intervallic relationships (see Jarman 1979: 81; Perle 1985: 85). Thus, the "dynamic curve" shape of many of these twelve-tone series (e.g., the basic series of *Lulu* or this of the *Lyric Suite*) suggests a deeply ingrained tendency. For examples of twelve-tone sets in Berg, see Jarman 1979, Chapter 3.

TABLE 5.5. Temporal location

Lower level	Peaks (n=84)		Controls (n=84)	
	%	n *	%	n *
1st quarter	14	(11.75)	21.4	(18)
1st note	2.3	(1.5)	1.2	(1)
2nd quarter	18.2	(15.25)	39.3	(33)
3rd quarter	25.8	(21.75)	16.7	(14)
Last quarter	42	(35.25)	22.6	(19)
Last note	18.5	(15.5)	1.2	(1)
1st half	32.2	(27)	60.7	(51)
2nd half	67.8	(57)	39.3	(33)
Outer half (1st + last q.)	56	(47)	44	(37)
Inner half (2nd + 3rd q.)	44	(37)	56	(47)

Middle level	Peaks (n=74)		Controls (n=71)	
	%	n	%	n
1st quarter	10.8	(8)	39.5	(28)
1st note	0	(0)	0	(0)
2nd quarter	8.1	(6)	22.5	(16)
3rd quarter	35.1	(26)	16.9	(12)
Last quarter	46	(34)	21.1	(15)
Last note	6.4	(3)	1.4	(1)
1st half	18.9	(14)	62	(44)
2nd half	81.1	(60)	38	(27)
Outer half (1st + last q.)	56.8	(42)	60.6	(43)
Inner half (2nd + 3rd q.)	43.2	(32)	39.4	(28)

Higher level	Peaks (n=49)		Controls (n=49)	
	%	n *	%	n *
1st quarter	6.1	(3)	28.6	(14)
1st note	0	(0)	0	(0)
2nd quarter	21	(10.3)	28.6	(14)
3rd quarter	32.3	(15.8)	26.5	(13)
Last quarter	40.6	(19.9)	16.3	(8)
Last note	0	(0)	0	(0)
1st half	27.1	(13.3)	57.2	(28)
2nd half	72.9	(35.7)	42.8	(21)
Outer half (1st + last q.)	46.7	(22.9)	44.9	(22)
Inner half (2nd + 3rd q.)	53.3	(26.1)	55.1	(27)

*See Table 3.5.

association with intervallic and durational stretches). Such patterns are often hierarchical, that is, several phrase groups, each built of an ascending pattern of lower-level arches, may themselves rise progressively and thus construct a higher-level ascending sequence of peaks. This organization partially explains the prevalence of late peaks at different levels of segmentation (see below, pp. 117–29).

The tendency to place melodic peaks late at diverse levels of segmentation points at the all-encompassing significance of "dynamic curve" processes in Berg's style, and suggests that melodic peaks, and melodic contour in general, often play an important role in shaping such processes in Berg. The strategies described above suggest how dynamic curves (insofar as they concern contour) are applied simultaneously and hierarchically to several segmental levels.

Prevalence of late climactic points (and of dynamic curves, associated with late climax) is usually assumed to be a typical nineteenth-century phenomenon. Of the three styles studied here, however, this post-Postromantic twentieth-century repertory exhibits these traits most strongly and most ubiquitously. As with other features (e.g., intervallic stretching) it seems that some gestural aspects of Romantic music receive their most intense expression in music that no longer shares their original syntactical framework.

Melodic Relationships

Both ascent toward and descent from peaks in the Berg repertory tend to be by large leaps. Isolated peaks, surrounded by large intervals, are thus characteristic of this repertory.

Intervals (Table 5.6). There is a highly significant difference ($\chi^2 = 23.51$, $p < .001$) between peaks and controls concerning approach intervals. Disjunct intervals are significantly more frequent in approaches to peaks ($z = 4.51$, $p < .001$). Intervals larger than a perfect fifth ($z = 3.51$, $p < .001$), Specifically sevenths ($z = 2.88$, $p < .01$), are particularly prominent in approaches.

Peaks and controls are also significantly different with regard to the intervals following them ($\chi^2 = 8.66$, $p < .02$). Noteworthy are the widest intervals—those larger than a perfect fifth ($z = 2.96$, $p < .01$), and in particular intervals exceeding the octave ($z = 2.77$, $p < .01$)—whose frequency in descents from peaks is significantly higher than in the controls.

There is a significant difference ($p < .01$) in the distribution of both ascending and descending intervals in the two groups (Table 5.7). Disjunct intervals as a whole are significantly more frequent at peaks in both directions ($z = 3.21$, $p < .002$ for ascents, $z = 2.12$, $p < .05$ for descents). Note in particular the high frequency of intervals larger than a perfect fifth ($z = 2.84$, $p < .005$ in ascents, $z = 3.59$, $p < .001$ in descents). Specifically, ascending sevenths ($z = 2.21$, $p < .05$) and descents larger than an octave ($z = 3.11$, $p < .002$) are significantly more frequent at peaks.

TABLE 5.6. Intervals

	I Intervals preceding peaks (n=83)		II Intervals following peaks (n=73)		III Intervals preceding controls (n=86)		IV Intervals following controls (n=85)		V Interval distribution − controls (III+IV) (n=171)	
	%	n	%	n	%	n	%	n	%	n
Seconds (m.-M.)	21.7	(18)	32.9	(24)	54.7	(47)	37.6	(32)	46.2	(79)
Augmented second	0	(0)	0	(0)	1.1	(1)	2.4	(2)	1.8	(3)
Thirds	18.1	(15)	11	(8)	14	(12)	22.3	(19)	18.1	(31)
Diminished fourth	0	(0)	1.4	(1)	0	(0)	3.5	(3)	1.8	(3)
Perfect fourth	10.8	(9)	12.3	(9)	11.6	(10)	9.4	(8)	10.5	(18)
Tritone	7.2	(6)	4.1	(3)	4.7	(4)	5.9	(5)	5.3	(9)
Perfect fifth	6	(5)	0	(0)	1.1	(1)	1.2	(1)	1.1	(2)
Sixths	7.2	(6)	5.5	(4)	3.5	(3)	4.7	(4)	4.1	(7)
Sevenths	16.9	(14)	8.2	(6)	3.5	(3)	7.1	(6)	5.3	(9)
Octave	2.4	(2)	4.1	(3)	1.1	(1)	0	(0)	.6	(1)
>Octave	9.6	(8)	20.5	(15)	4.7	(4)	5.9	(5)	5.3	(9)
All disjunct intervals (>seconds)										
	78.3	(65)	67.1	(49)	44.2	(38)	60	(51)	52	(89)
>Perfect fifth	36.1	(30)	38.4	(28)	12.8	(11)	17.6	(15)	15.2	(26)

Melodic emphasis (Table 5.8). The difference between peaks and controls in melodic emphasis is highly significant ($\chi^2 = 26.9$, $p < .001$) for relations with earlier neighbors, but only marginally significant ($\chi^2 = 7.24$, $p < .05$) for relations with later neighbors. Cases in which later neighbors are more emphasized than the preceding peaks (the minus row) are almost as common as cases in which the peaks are more emphasized (the plus row). The different relations to earlier and later neighbors reflect the tendency to approach and leave peaks with large intervals, thus isolating them registrally. While Such registrally isolated peaks are themselves strongly marked for attention, the fall from them also marks the following note, which frequently has a closural function. Thus, such peaks are commonly parts of a cadential pattern (see "terminal fall" below). Still, as Table 5.8 indicates (at "relations with both neighbors"), nearly half of the examined peaks are melodically emphasized relative to both their neighbors, while this is the case only in a small minority (11.3%) of the controls, a difference that is highly significant statistically ($z = 4.93$, $p < .001$).

Table 5.7. Ascending versus descending intervals

Intervals	Peaks— ascending (n=83)		Controls— ascending (n=84)		Peaks— descending (n=73)		Controls— descending (n=87)	
	%	n	%	n	%	n	%	n
Seconds	21.7	(18)	45.2	(38)	32.9	(24)	49.4	(43)
Thirds	18.1	(15)	27.4	(23)	12.4	(9)	12.6	(11)
Perfect fourth	10.8	(9)	7.1	(6)	12.3	(9)	13.8	(12)
Tritone	7.2	(6)	3.6	(3)	4.1	(3)	8	(7)
Perfect fifth	6	(5)	0	(0)	0	(0)	2.3	(2)
Sixths	7.2	(6)	4.8	(4)	5.5	(4)	3.4	(3)
Sevenths	16.9	(14)	6	(5)	8.2	(6)	4.6	(4)
Octave	2.4	(2)	0	(0)	4.1	(3)	1.1	(1)
> Octave	9.6	(8)	6	(5)	20.5	(15)	4.6	(4)
All disjunct intervals (>seconds)								
	78.3	(65)	54.8	(46)	67.1	(49)	50.6	(44)
>Perfect fifth	36.1	(30)	16.7	(14)	38.4	(28)	13.8	(12)

Table 5.8. Melodic emphasis

	Peaks		Controls	
	%	n	%	n
RELATION WITH EARLIER NEIGHBOR				
+	67.5	(54)	26.8	(22)
=	8.7	(7)	22	(18)
−	23.8	(19)	51.2	(42)
Total n		(80)		(82)
RELATION WITH LATER NEIGHBOR				
+	47.1	(33)	32.9	(28)
=	10	(7)	20	(17)
−	42.9	(30)	47.1	(40)
Total n		(70)		(85)
SELECTED RELATIONS WITH BOTH NEIGHBORS				
++	41.8	(28)	11.3	(9)
= =	4.5	(3)	12.5	(10)

Melodic Patterns

The following discussion interprets the intervallic statistics in Tables 5.6–5.8, and goes beyond what can be directly inferred from these statistical results. The discussion is divided into two parts. The first concerns the local, foreground intervallic gestures typically associated with melodic peaks in the Berg repertory. The second deals with the pitch- and contour configurations connecting different peaks.

Local Gestures

Terminal fall. Perhaps the most conspicuous of the local melodic gestures associated with peaks in the Berg sample is a large downward skip from a melodic peak at the end of a phrase or a section. Such terminal falls—sometimes a decisive leap through the entire vocal range, sometimes a *portamento*, occasionally two or three successive downward skips—are particularly prevalent in *Lulu*, where they are featured at the conclusion of important sections and dramatically consequential phrases. Falls, for instance, end the last phrases of both scenes of the opera's second act, creating an ironic parallelism: at the end of the first scene the fall is Lulu's pleading scream to Alwa, begging him to take her with him and to save her from arrest for his father's murder (see measure 647 in Example 5.5); at the end of the second scene (and of the entire act) Alwa's resignation to Lulu is illustrated by similar gestures (Example 5.8, measures 1135–36, 1142–43). These and other such gestures in the opera (e.g., those in act I measure 175, or act II measures 330, 903–905) perform both expressive and structural functions. They are expressive of extreme agitation or excitement (perhaps by their naturalistic suggestion of agitated speech) and provide a strong sign of closure by "summing up" an entire vocal range, falling from its very top to its bottom. Thus these gestures function to create conspicuous emphasis—both rhetorical and grammatical.[6]

Gap-fill. Gap-fill patterns are strongly associated with melodic peaks in tonal—particularly nineteenth century—music[7] Peaks in Berg's nontonal music, however, also present conspicuous examples of "perfect" gap-fill schemata—immediate, direct, and complete conjunct fills of large intervallic gaps, as in Examples 5.9 and 5.10. In such cases, Berg seems to borrow a prevalent Romantic melodic gesture and implant it, often in an exaggerated form, outside its original tonal context.

The gap-fill schema is particularly fit for such implantation. Though this pattern has usually been discussed in relation to tonal or modal music, it is not necessarily related to tonal syntax. Rather, gap-fill may be interpreted as a universal tension-resolution gesture, based on "natural," cross-stylistic tensional connotations of con-

6. For a different view of such gestures see Narmour's discussion of Registral Reversal (VR) structures (1990: Chapter 20).

7. See Meyer 1989, Chapter 7 (especially pp. 245–58), and Chapter 4 of the present book.

EXAMPLE 5.8. Berg, *Lulu*, Act II, Scene 2, measures 1130–1150. Copyright 1936 by Universal Edition, A.G., Vienna.

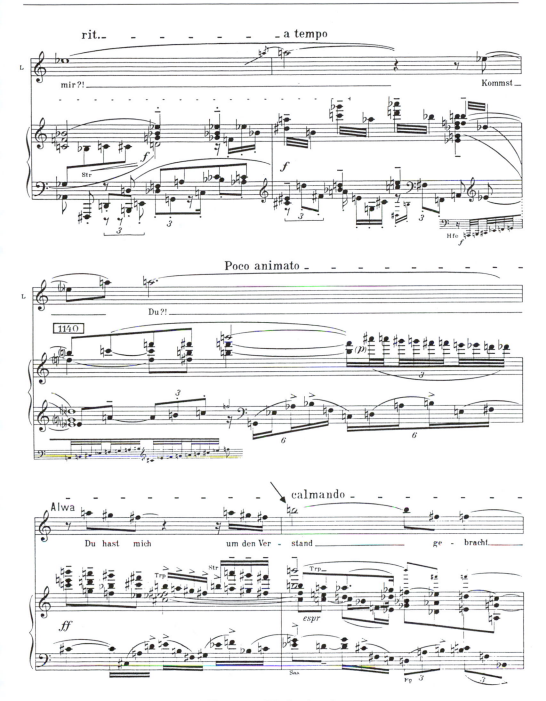

EXAMPLE 5.8. Continued.

EXAMPLE 5.8. Continued.

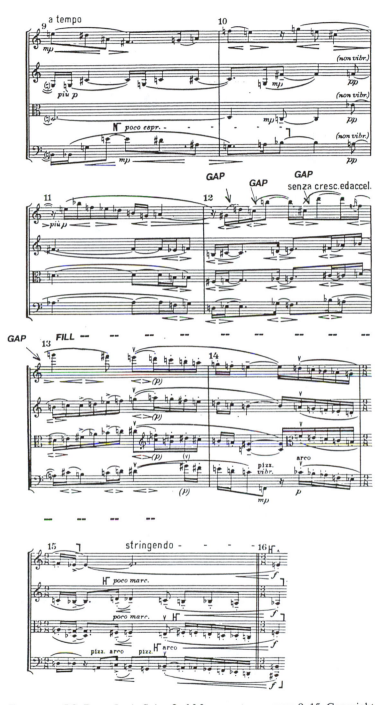

EXAMPLE 5.9. Berg, *Lyric Suite*, 2nd Movement, measures 9–15. Copyright 1927, renewed 1954 by Universal Edition, A.G., Vienna.

EXAMPLE 5.10. Berg, *Lulu*, Act II, Scene 1, Measures 1009–1015. Copyright 1936 by Universal Edition, A.G., Vienna.

tour and interval size:[8] both pitch ascent and large intervals seem (as psychological and speech-intonation studies suggest; see chapter 1) to be cross-culturally and extra-musically associated with increased tension; correspondingly, descending pitch and small intervals relieve tension. Thus, following a large ascending leap with smaller descending progressions releases tension, regardless of tonal syntax.

Such nonsyntactic view of the gap-fill schema may account for its prevalence in posttonal contexts such as Berg's, where Meyer's notions of melodic completeness or structural gaps do not easily apply.[9] Moreover, so viewed, gap-fill patterns do not demand a conjunct fill, but merely a fill by descending intervals smaller than the gap-opening ascent. Thus, though large leaps to a melodic peak in Berg are commonly followed by smaller descending intervals, these intervals are often themselves leaps (see, e.g., Example 5.11, as well as the opening measures of the same movement, Example 5.2). In an even more frequent variant of the gesture, often serving a quasi-cadential function, a single descent of a minor second, leading to a sustained tone (rather than an actual fill of the melodic gap), serves to balance a tensional skip to a peak (Example 5.12, measures 95–96 (1st violin), 98–100 (viola), 100–101 (cello)).

Gap-fill formations are comparable to other devices in Berg's music that draw upon Romantic or Postromantic music without employing its tonal syntax, for example the use of melodic and rhythmic stretching, of tertial chord morphologies and quasi-tonal harmonic progressions, or even the literal quotations of Wagner (the *Tristan* motive) and Zemlinsky in the *Lyric Suite*. Often, allusions to harmonic and melodic Romantic gestures work hand in hand. In Example 5.13, for instance, the use of "thickened" triadic progressions complements the gap-fill patterns in the vocal

8. For examples of cross-cultural uses of gap-fill gestures, see Meyer 1956: 131–32.

9. The above notion of gap-fill differs from Meyer's original explanation, 1956, based upon the notion of melodic incompleteness:

> In the music of a culture the tonal materials given in the style system establish a norm of melodic completeness. That is, in any tonal system there is a normal repertory of tones which mark off the distance between tones of equivalence or duplication, usually the octave. The total complement of such tones constitutes completeness for the system. When the practiced or cultivated listener becomes aware that one of these steps has been passed over (left out) he expects, albeit unconsciously, that the missing tone will be forthcoming later in the series. He expects, that is, that the structural gaps created by such a skip will eventually be filled in. (p. 131)

I doubt whether a listener hearing a melodic skip in Berg's posttonal repertory perceives (as the chromatic aggregate constitute the "repertory of tones" in this music) the intervening chromatic notes as "missing," and hence expects a chromatic fill of this skip (indeed, the gradual completion of the chromatic aggregate is a common strategy in posttonal music, but this completion is usually achieved in ways that have little to do with gap-fill patterns). Meyer himself currently holds the view (close to that expressed here) that gap-fill patterns are not syntactic scripts, specifying exact "slots" to be filled. Rather, they are plan-like schemata (perhaps grounded in universal motor/muscular proclivities), that do not specify the pitches that constitute completeness, and are not dependent on tonal syntax.

For a different "universalist" view of the implications of large leaps see Narmour's notion of "reversal" (1990).

Example 5.11. Berg, *Lyric Suite*, 4th Movement, measures 24–27. Copyright 1927, renewed 1954 by Universal Edition, A.G., Vienna.

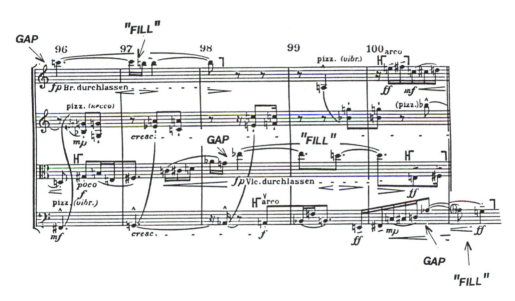

EXAMPLE 5.12. Berg, *Lyric Suite*, 2nd Movement, measures 92–101. Copyright 1927, renewed 1954 by Universal Edition, A.G., Vienna.

line. Thus, the underlying Gb harmony gives the B⁵ peak in measure 1001 the status of an elongated appoggiatura—a typical configuration in much nineteenth-century music.[10] The peak at the ensuing measure 1010 (Example 5.10) functions similarly, as a kind of seventh in a Db major chord. Such fusion of melodic and harmonic Romantic gestures within a foreign, posttonal environment is a substantial component of Berg's style.

10. See Meyer 1989: 264, 281–83.

EXAMPLE 5.13. Berg, *Lulu*, Act II, Scene 1, measures 1000–1004. Copyright 1936 by Universal Edition, A.G., Vienna.

Contour and Pitch Relationships Among Peaks

Important as the intervallic gestures at melodic peaks are, the higher-level configurations of pitches, intervals, and contours that relate successive peaks to one another are of no lesser significance. Though such relationships are not directly addressed in my statistical analysis, their importance in Berg's music merits at least a brief consideration.

In the following discussion, I first address typical low-level configurations of melodic peaks, and the strategy of intervallic stretching commonly associated with such configurations. Then, examples of peak-relationships over a larger scale are given, and techniques by which such larger-scale relationships are brought to the surface are discussed. Finally, I discuss cases in which the pitch patterns created among peaks themselves have a structural, quasi-thematic significance.

Low-level peak patterns; intervallic stretching. Relationships among successive peaks are perhaps most conspicuous at low and intermediate levels of segmentation, namely, within phrases or phrase groups. Particularly prominent at these levels (especially in climactic or extremely agitated segments) are ascending series of peaks, which create a clear, directed motion toward a higher, more emphatic apex. Such ascents (as in Example 5.5) are often associated with sequential, or quasi-sequential, melodic progressions, a practice much indebted to nineteenth-century Romanticism.

Both durational and intervallic stretching, which are prominent in many series of ascending peaks, strengthen the association of melodic peaks with climactic emphasis by relating rise in register with the strengthening of agogic and intervallic emphases. The use of durational stretching in an ascending peak pattern was discussed in connection with Example 5.5. Example 5.14 illustrates the intricate use of intervallic stretching in such a configuration.

In this example, the ascending peak pattern E^5 (viola, measure 8), G^5 (second violin, measure 10), Bb^5 (first violin, measure 12), C^6 (measure 12), Eb^6 (measure 13), $F\#^6$ (measure 13) is first brought forth by imitative statements of the movement's principal motive in the viola (measures 7–9) and the second violin (measures 9–11), and continues in an ascending series of abbreviated and intervallically stretched versions of this motive in the first violin, culminating in measure 13. In this structure, intervallic stretching is employed at two levels: within melodic figures, and among them. The viola and second violin figures at measures 7–11, both variants of the movement's opening figure (see Example 5.2), begin, like the original motive, with a minor second. This intervallic standard is progressively stretched, creating wedge-shaped figures culminating with major seventh leaps to the highpoint. On a higher level, intervallic stretching is employed among successive figures, affecting ascents toward and descents from peaks. Ascents are stretched from major sevenths (F^4 to E^5 [viola] and Ab^4 to G^5 [second violin], measures 8 and 10) to a perfect eleventh (F^4 to Bb^5 [first violin], measures 11–12), a minor thirteenth (E^4 to C^6, measure 12), and finally the gargantuan interval of a diminished seventeenth ($C\#^4$ to Eb^6, measures 12–13). Then (measures 12–13) the descents from peaks are also stretched, from a moderate stepwise descent (Bb to Ab, C to B, measure 12) to a steep fall, constituted of two large intervals (first a diminished fifth plus a perfect fifth, then a minor seventh plus an augmented fifth, in measure 13 [first violin]).

In Example 5.9, an ascending series of local peaks produces a progressive process of durational and intervallic stretching, combined with a gradual heightening of metric emphasis. This process, culminating at the G^6 peak at measure 13, is outlined in Table 5.9.

Stretching and its association with series of ascending melodic peaks are typical nineteenth-century gestures.[11] Berg, however, does not simply transplant these gestures into a posttonal environment: his attitude toward them is complex and contradictory. Examples 5.9 and 5.14 illustrate two contrasting facets of Berg's treatment of

---

11. See Meyer 1989: 260–69 for examples.

EXAMPLE 5.14. Berg, *Lyric Suite*, 4th Movement, measures 7–14. Copyright 1927, renewed 1954 by Universal Edition, A.G., Vienna.

TABLE 5.9. Progressive emphasis in the *Lyric Suite*, 2nd movement, measures 9–15

Peak pitch	Measure	Metric location	Duration	Approaching interval
G⁵	10	off beat	sixteenth note	m3
B♭⁵	11	up-beat	sixteenth note	dim. 5
B⁵	12	up-beat	dotted eighth note	M7
D⁶	12	up-beat	dotted eighth note	m9
G⁶	13	downbeat	quarter note	M9

this prevalent Romantic gesture. The first, present in both examples, is the exaggeration of the gesture. The second, shown in Example 5.9, is the denial of its climactic implications.

The sense in which Berg uses manic "hyperstretches" is, here and elsewhere, the result of several factors. First, the intervals themselves are huge, even in the context of Berg's melodic style. In particular, the intervallic standard against which the stretch is measured is itself sometimes a very large leap, as in Example 5.14, where the stretch expands a major seventh. Second, stretches often occur as part of an intensifying series of successive stretches. Third, the final, most extreme stretches in the series are often condensed into a short time-span (e.g., measures 12–13 in Example 5.9, measures 11–13 in Example 5.14), thus suggesting a manic loss of control.

The progressive intensification of stretches, however, often fails to reach the implied climax. The process tabulated for Example 5.9 seems to be leading naturally toward a powerful "structural highpoint" at measure 13. This potential climax, however, never materializes. Berg counteracts climactic implications here by explicit performance directions and by the progression of the lower voices. In measure 12, where a quick succession of intervallic and durational stretches in the 1st violin part implies an impending climax, Berg directs "*senza crescendo ed accelerando,*" thus warning against the tendency to support the gradual intensification of contour intervals with intensification of dynamics and pace—a "natural," though misguided, performance reaction to such a situation.[12] *Crescendo* and *stringendo* indications appear instead near the end of the long, stepwise descent at measure 15, again negating "natural" performance tendencies toward abatement. In addition, the three lower voices counteract the upper line's potentially powerful downbeat in measure 13, emphasizing instead the second beat of the measure.

Such a complex and equivocal relation to typical Romantic gestures—affirming them strongly while negating their implications—contributes significantly to the expressive intensity of Berg's music. The investigation of peak relations in general, and of stretching among peaks in particular, may thus bear on a central and relatively neglected aspect of Berg's expressive design.

---

12. Agawu 1982; Berry 1976; Hopkins 1990; Meyer 1989; Nakamura 1987; and Sheer 1989, among others, discuss such parametric parallelism.

EXAMPLE 5.15A. Berg, *Lulu*, Act I, Scene 1, measures 334–339. Copyright 1936 by Universal Edition, A.G., Vienna

EXAMPLE 5.15B. Berg, *Lulu*, Act I, Scene 1, measures 348–350. Copyright 1936 by Universal Edition, A.G., Vienna

More distant peak relationships; peak prolongation. Conspicuous relations among peaks are not confined to the lowest levels of segmentation. Motivic relations, as well as strategies emphasizing peaks and isolating them from their surroundings, often create clearly perceptible registral connections (frequently linear or tertial) between rather distant melodic peaks. For instance, the B^5 peak in Example 5.15b (measure 349) may be clearly perceived as continuing the linear pattern of ascending peaks ($F\sharp^5$, $A\flat^5$, $B\flat^5$, highlighting a repetition of "Wach auf") from Example 5.15a (measures 336–339). This connection is highlighted by motivic similarity (the ascending minor seventh), as well as by the low vocal registration in the measures preceding the B^5 peak.

Berg often uses peak "prolongation" to create registral connections. Strong durational emphasis, motivic similarity, or registral isolation relates two peaks of the same pitch, making them stand apart from the surrounding notes. Such prolongation is sometimes followed by an immediate ascent to a higher melodic apex. The concluding phrases of "Die Seele der Weines," the first song in *Der Wein* (Example 5.16) exemplify this strategy. The section opens with an F^5 peak (voice part, measure 73),

EXAMPLE 5.16. Berg, *Der Wein*, *Die Seele Der Weines*, measures 72–84. Copyright 1951 by Universal Edition, A.G., Vienna.

strongly emphasized by duration, a large leap (a major sixth), dynamics (an orchestral *crescendo*), and a marked change in orchestration and texture. It ends with a reiteration of the same peak pitch (measure 80), followed by a further ascent to A^5. The connection between those two points is underscored by the durational emphasis that separates both from their surroundings, and it is strengthened by partial similarity of pitch progression (note the salience of the A♭ [G♯]–F relation in both cases, as well as the similar "triadic" settings in both).

EXAMPLE 5.16. Continued.

EXAMPLE 5.16. Continued.

A more complex instance of peak prolongation is in the fourth movement of the *Lyric Suite* (Examples 5.17a, 5.17b). The first section of this movement is built of three processes of intensification and abatement (measures 1–7, 7–14, 14–24). Each of these segments reiterates the peak pitches of the preceding one, and then ascends to a higher peak. Thus, the peak pattern C^6–$E\flat$ $(D\sharp)^6$ at measures 5–6[13] is reiterated in measures 12–13, followed by a further ascent to $F\sharp^6$; the C^6–$E\flat^6$–$F\sharp^6$ configura-

13. Though E6 is the actual melodic peak in measure 6, the following D♯ is clearly more prominent, due primarily to its durational and metric distinction.

EXAMPLE 5.17A. Berg, *Lyric Suite*, 4th movement, measures 1–24. Copyright 1927, renewed 1954 by Universal Edition, A.G., Vienna.

EXAMPLE 5.17.A Continued.

EXAMPLE 5.17.A Continued.

EXAMPLE 5.17.A Continued.

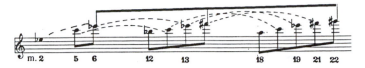

EXAMPLE 5.17B. Registral connections in Example 5.17a.

tion reappears at the peak of the next arch (measures 19–21), followed by an ascent to a higher peak, G$\sharp^6$ (measure 22). This peak prolongation, outlining a large-scale process of graded ascent, holds together an extensive section.

Pitch patterns in series of peaks. A further indication of the structural importance of peak patterns are the perceptible "motives" they sometimes create. What makes such patterns noteworthy is the striking affinity they sometimes exhibit to prominent surface motives or pitch cells.

In Examples 5.18 and 5.19, the peak progression in a section constitutes a large-scale version of its salient surface progressions. In Example 5.18 the same chromatic figure unfolds simultaneously as a near-surface level and a "higher-level" progression of melodic peaks. Each figure of the first violin line in this segment ascends to a peak situated a minor second higher than that of the previous figure, thus establishing an ascending chromatic progression of peaks (from B^5 to B^6). At the same time, each of these figures itself presents a near-surface version of the same ascending chromatic progression, featured by the higher line in a kind of bilevel melodic configuration (see Example 5.18b).[14] To further emphasize the peaks-surface relation, at the end of the section (measure 67) the chromatic progression from F^6 to B^6, which constitutes the later part of the preceding peak sequence, is brought to the very surface. Another correspondence between peak progression and a note-to-note pattern occurs in the last section in the fourth movement of the *Lyric Suite* (Examples 5.19a, b). The section exhibits a conspicuous three-note peak pattern: its first two statements (Example 5.19a, measures 59–62, 62–65) open with salient ascents to B$\flat^5$ and C^6, respectively, and the last statement (Example 5.19b, measures 66–69) presents a gradual ascent to a terminal C$\sharp^6$ peak. This final segment consists of a series of three-note stepwise ascents, each composed—like the B$\flat$–C–C$\sharp$ pattern of melodic peaks—of a minor and a major second (see circled figures in Examples 5.19a, b). The last of these three-note cells—the terminal melodic progression in the movement (first violin, measures 67–69)—presents the progression A$\sharp^5$–B$\sharp^5$–C$\sharp^6$, the same figure that has simultaneously been unfolding as a peak pattern. The peak figure is thus precisely corresponds—first intervallically, then with its exact pitches—to the note-to-note level.

Such relationships are not unique.[15] Together with other structural functions

14. These figures are derived from the opening (and principal) motive of the movement (measures 2–3). Thus, the peak progression here is a large-scale projection not only of a concurrent figure, but also of the movement's principal thematic figure. Perle (1985: 16–17) also refers to the chromatic progression imbedded at the movement's main motive, pointing out a rhythmic motive brought forth by this pattern.

15. Ex. 5.15a presents another case of such parallelism: note the peak progression E$\flat$–F$\sharp$–G$\sharp$, replicated near the surface in measures 19–22. Among other cases, of particular interest is the projection of

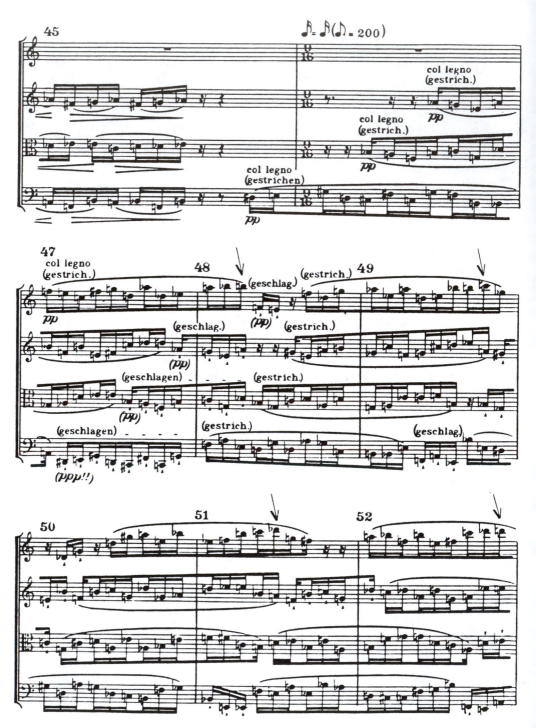

EXAMPLE 5.18A. Berg, *Lyric Suite*, 3rd Movement, measures 45–69. Copyright 1927, renewed 1954 by Universal Edition, A.G., Vienna.

EXAMPLE 5.18.A Continued.

EXAMPLE 5.18.A Continued.

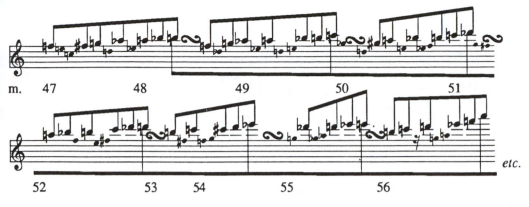

m.   47   48   49   50   51

52   53   54   55   56

etc.

EXAMPLE 5.18B. Bi-level chromatic progression in Example 5.18a.

of contour the treatment of peak patterns as long-range, spread-out motives, cor-responding to prominent "surface" pitch cells, attests to the signal importance in Berg's music of contoural gestures, particularly those associated with the melodic peak phenomenon.[16]

Repeated pitches (Table 5.10, p. 131). Configurations of repeated pitches are not associated with peaks in the Berg sample.

Pitch-register singularity (Table 5.11). As in the other two repertories, there is a strong tendency ($z = 5.48, p < .001$ in low-level segments; $z = 7.36, p < .001$ in larger sections) to avoid presenting a peak-pitch more than once: few of Berg's peak-pitches are repeated, either in shorter segments or in larger sections.[17] At the lower levels of segmentation, this tendency has a near-rule status. Not only were few peak pitches presented more than once in phrase-level melodic lines; the few exceptions almost always involve a repetition of the entire figure of which the peaks are a part (similar to the Haydn and Chopin repertories). Because the peak recurs in the same context, such repetition does not detract much from the impression of singularity. Rather, repetition often serves to extend a melodic highpoint, thus placing extra emphasis on a signifi-cant point in the melodic discourse. This is the case in the concluding phrase of the *Lyric Suite* (Example 5.20, measures 42–43, 1st violin), where the final statement of the movement's opening motive (in its original form; compare mm. 42–43 with the movement's opening notes) and a last touch in the higher register are marked by a triple repetition of the melodic peak.

"triadic" peak patterns in the first two movements of the *Lyric Suite*. The "major triad" configuration Ab (measure 3)–C (measures 8–11)–Eb (measure 12) is prominent in the beginning of the exposition of the first movement, and the same pitch classes reappear around the exposition's peak (measures 25–27), this time near the surface.

16. Perle's examples of the linear motion created by the outer voices of bilevel lines, and of inter-vallic and rhythmic cells outlined by such outer voices (actually, local peaks) are also relevant to the present discussion (1985: 17, 194, 210).

17. Note, however, that in a considerable proportion of controls (though fewer than in the peaks) pitch repetition was also avoided. The reasons, particularly for the dodecaphonic pieces, are obvious.

EXAMPLE 5.19A. Berg, *Lyric Suite*, 4th Movement, measures 59–65. Copyright 1927, renewed 1954 by Universal Edition, A.G., Vienna.

The singularity of peak pitches extends to the highest levels of segmentation, sometimes even the entire piece. Often, such unique pitches are situated at a climactic point near the very end of a piece or movement. In *Der Wein*, the highest pitch in the vocal part, $A\sharp^5$, is featured once in the entire piece, as the second to last note in the vocal line (measure 207; see Example 5.4). In the *Four Pieces for Clarinet and Piano*, none of the pitches in the chromatic figure that is the melodic apex of the last movement and of the whole piece (E^6, F^6, $F\sharp^6$, G^6, measure 16, clarinet part) are used anywhere else in the clarinet part. And the melodic peaks in two scenes of the second act of *Lulu*, both situated at climactic points near the scene's end ($C\sharp^6$, measure 647,[18]

18. There is a higher peak earlier in that scene (D6, measures 220–21), which also appears once only in the scene. This peak is, however, optional (an alternative descent to D5 is offered), unlike the later C6♯ highpoint.

EXAMPLE 5.19B. Berg, *Lyric Suite*, 4th Movement, measures 66–69. Copyright 1927, renewed 1954 by Universal Edition, A.G., Vienna.

TABLE 5.10. Repeated pitches

	Peaks (n=97)		Controls (n=100)	
	%	n	%	n
Repeated	11.6	(10)	12.7	(11)
Not repeated	88.2	(79)	87.3	(78)

TABLE 5.11. Pitch-register singularity

	Peaks (n=86)		Controls (n=86)	
	%	n	%	n
In low-level segment (5–10 measures)	84.9	(73)	45.3	(39)
In section	76.7	(66)	20.9	(18)

D^6, measure 1084), use pitches that do not occur in the vocal parts anywhere else in the scene.

What are the functions of this all-encompassing strategy? As already suggested, uniqueness of pitch/register at the peak may enhance our sense of its importance and tends to create a distinctive and memorable melodic profile, especially when (as is often the case in this repertory) the melodic line thrusts upward toward a peak, or when a progressively heightening series of arches shapes a melody. In such cases, the

*) bis zum völligen Verlöschen, daher die letzte Terz *Des - F* eventuell noch ein-, zweimal wiedor-
holen. Keinesfalls aber auf *Des* schließen!

EXAMPLE 5.20. Berg, *Lyric Suite*, 6th Movement, measures 39–46. Copyright 1927, renewed 1954 by
Universal Edition, A.G., Vienna.

TABLE 5.12. Dynamic emphasis

	Peaks (n=86)		Controls (n=86)	
	%	n	%	n
Processive (end of cresc.)	30.2	(26)	4.7	(4)
Local (accent, *Sfz*)	16.3	(14)	9.3	(8)

uniqueness of the peak-pitch enhances its perception as a goal or climax of melodic motion, and as a result may highlight the entire phrase of which it is a part. In addition, the distinctive profile intensified by a unique peak-pitch may (as we have seen) support registral connections among peaks in different segments. In lieu of the support of tonal implication, strategies such as these become very important in enhancing long-range continuity and a clear sense of goal-directedness.

DYNAMICS

Dynamic emphases (Table 5.12). Ascent in pitch is correlated with dynamic increase in Berg, as it is in Chopin. Berg's melodic peaks, often situated at the end of a *crescendo*, are significantly correlated with peaks of dynamic processes ($z = 4.47, p < .001$). As in the Chopin sample, peaks are not significantly associated with local stress, such as *sforzando* ($z = 1.38, p > .05$).

In Examples 5.2 (p. 90) and 5.21, the openings of the fourth and sixth movements of the *Lyric Suite*, Berg clearly and effectively uses the natural correlation between pitch ascent and increase in dynamics (accompanied an increase in textural density) to emphasize the culmination point, the peak of several parallel processes.[19]

PARAMETRIC INTERACTION

Combined parametric emphasis (Table 5.13). This summary category indicates the strong inclination in the Berg repertory to present peaks emphatically, combining durational, metric, and intervallic means. There is a highly significant difference ($\chi^2 = 29.9, p < .001$) between peaks and controls in distribution of the four degrees of combined emphasis. Particularly, the "high emphasis" category is far more frequent

19. Note that here as elsewhere Berg's Expressionistic idiom combines this straightforward adherence to some "natural" processes with a sophisticated manipulation of others. In Example 5.19, for instance, the clear parallel processes of pitch ascent and dynamic increase are accompanied by a contradictory rhythmic process, in which an extreme deceleration in tempo accompanies a marked acceleration of notated surface rhythm. When this contradiction explodes in measures 7–8, the result is a marked fall in tempo and density at the very height of dynamic, contoural, and intervallic intensification.

EXAMPLE 5.21. Berg, *Lyric Suite*, 6th Movement, measures 1–8. Copyright 1927, renewed 1954 by Universal Edition, A.G., Vienna.

TABLE 5.13. Combined parametric emphasis

	Peaks (n=86)		Controls (n=86)	
	%	n	%	n
High (4–6)	33.7	(29)	9	(8)
Medium-high (1–3)	36	(32)	23.6	(20)
Medium-low (−2–0)	20.2	(17)	38.2	(32)
Low (−6–3)	10.1	(8)	29.2	(26)

at peaks, while the "low emphasis" class is considerably less frequent there. Many of the examples discussed in this chapter (e.g., Examples 5.1 5.2, 5.10, 5.21) demonstrate cases of such "high emphasis:" combinations of a long, sometimes extreme duration, metric accent, and a large approaching skip (among other things) that make a strongly emphatic peak.

Interparametric congruence (Tables 5.14–5.16). The relation between metric and melodic (intervallic) emphases in Berg's music (Table 5.15) calls attention to the one difference between peaks and controls in inter-parametric congruence.[20] Peaks show significant congruence between these two parameters ($\chi^2 = 8.89$, $p < .01$); in other words, larger skips around peaks tend to head toward points of metric accent. In contrast, no significant metric-melodic congruence appears in the control group ($\chi^2 = 2.59$, $p > .05$). This trait is, then, specific to melodic peaks.

Such congruence of interval size, contour, and meter is a noteworthy characteristic of prominent thematic and climactic statements. For instance, consistent congruence among these elements shapes the principal motive of the *Lyric Suite*'s first movement (Example 5.1, measures 2–3, first violin): in each pair of successive notes in this motive (E^4–C^5, A^5–G^5, D^5–Ab^5), the higher one is metrically accented and approached by a larger interval (see also the principal motive of the 4th movement, Example 5.2). The opening measures of the "Prolog" to *Lulu* (Example 5.22) exhibit a similar congruence, though not on such a minute level (note the peaks of the trombone and trumpet motives in the downbeats of measures 2 and 4, respectively). Such congruent relations can be part of a piece's *Grundgestalt*, carried forward, as an initial gestural "premise" to statements not directly related to the opening motive.[21]

No difference between peaks and controls was discerned in durational-metric and durational-melodic congruencies. Peaks and controls alike exhibit a highly significant degree of congruence between metric and durational emphases; neither group shows a significant congruence between durational and melodic emphases.

20. Other results of χ^2 tests for parametric congruence are as follows. In metric-durational congruence: peaks—$\chi^2 = 30.6$, $p < .001$; control—$\chi^2 = 28.75$, $p < .001$. In durational-melodic congruence: peaks—$\chi^2 = 1.1$, $p > .05$; control—$\chi^2 = 3.52$, $p > .05$.

21. For discussions of initial gestural "premises" in nineteenth-century compositions, See Eitan 1995 and Hatten 1993.

TABLE 5.14. Congruence between metric and durational emphases

Meter	Duration					
	Peaks			Controls		
	+	−		+	−	
+	70 (60.7)	3 (12.3)	73	27 (16.5)	7 (17.5)	34
−	14 (23.3)	14 (4.7)	28	3 (13.5)	25 (14.5)	28
	84	17	101	30	32	62

TABLE 5.15. Congruence between metric and melodic emphases

Meter	Melody					
	Peaks			Controls		
	+	−		+	−	
+	55 (48.8)	13 (19.2)	68	16 (12.4)	22 (25.7)	38
−	16 (22.2)	15 (8.8)	31	15 (18.6)	42 (38.4)	57
	71	28	99	31	64	95

TABLE 5.16. Congruence between durational and melodic emphases

Duration	Melody					
	Peaks			Controls		
	+	−		+	−	
+	60 (58)	29 (31)	89	15 (11.3)	14 (19.7)	29
−	11 (13)	9 (7)	20	10 (13.7)	25 (22.3)	35
	71	38	109	25	39	64

CONCLUSION

Peaks in Berg are often—as postulated in my initial hypotheses—points of strong emphasis, culminations of intensifying processes. More often and more emphatically than in the two earlier repertories, melodic peaks are expressive and structural high-points. This is evident in both their local and their global relationships. Locally, peaks in Berg are significantly associated with extreme durational emphasis, metric accents, large intervals (in both motion toward and away from peaks), and the culmination of

EXAMPLE 5.22. Berg, *Lulu*, Prolog, measures 1–8. Copyright 1936 by Universal Edition, A.G., Vienna.

crescendi. Globally, the peak pitch is often unique within the piece or within a large section of it (as are, at times, some of its attributes, such as its duration or the intervals approaching it); it typically appears near the end of a section; and it is frequently prepared by an ascending and progressively stretched series of lesser peaks.

These characteristics suggest that Berg often used the "natural" shaping force and connotations of contour peaks as a compositional tool. As I have shown, the emphatic and tensional connotations of peaks make them useful in two structurally important ways: as local signs of impending closure and as the climaxes of long-range processes of intensification. Further, the emphatic force of peaks significantly enhances continuity by establishing long-range pitch connections, and at times facilitates the emergence of high-level motives. While such strategies have also played a significant role in earlier, tonal music, they seem even more important in this post-tonal repertory, where the long-range voice leading and harmonic relationships that tonality enables are not available. Lacking the directional means supplied by tonal syntax, Berg relies on nonsyntactic aspects of melody, particularly contour, to create a clear, goal-directed melodic structure. Thus, strategies used in earlier (particularly nineteenth-century) music to support tonal directionality may become here a chief carrier of melodic direction—which explains the amplified manner in which contoural gestures are often featured in Berg.

Indeed, a striking facet of Berg's handling of peaks is an unmistakable suggestion of Romantic gestures. Comparisons with the Chopin analysis in chapter 4 and outside evidence suggest that Berg's use of melodic contour resembles that of some nineteenth-century Romantic music. With regard to nearly all the characteristics investigated, results in the Chopin and Berg repertories are highly similar, with contour peaks functioning as emphatic and tensional points of climax. Further, some important configurations and processes utilizing peaks in Berg are characteristic of nineteenth-century music: these include the tendency to place peaks late in sections and the hierarchy of dynamic curves with which that tendency is associated;[22] stretching, a hallmark of nineteenth-century melodic expression, and gap-fill structures.

These Romantic allusions bear on an important and problematic facet of Berg's musical idiom. It has often been suggested that Berg's music, perhaps more than most posttonal music, is a continuation and expansion of nineteenth-century idioms. Accordingly, his music is sometimes perceived as an incoherent tonal-attonal compromise, a kind of muddled version of serialism and a corruption of its modernist ideals.[23] Recent analyses by Perle, Jarman, and others, however, convincingly show that the organization of pitch (and other parameters) in Berg is permeated by untraditional organizational procedures, as remote from these of nineteenth-century Romanticism as those of his two Viennese contemporaries.[24]

What relates Berg's music (including pieces such as *Lulu*, in which, according to Jarman (1979: 223) "almost every musical parameter is affected by some kind of precompositionally determined scheme,") so clearly to nineteenth-century modes of expression? Discussions of the traditional aspects of Berg's music usually concentrate

22. See Agawu 1982, Meyer 1989 for relevant nineteenth-century analyses.

23. This has been particularly the view of the post-Schönberg European avant-garde, most bluntly expressed by Boulez.

24. For instance, the harmonic and melodic manipulation of "tropes" (unordered segments of the twelve-tone rows), the association of different rows used in the same piece (by using of the same tropes in different rows, or through cyclical permutations of the original set, among other means. See Perle 1980 and Jarman 1979, chapter 6). In Berg's late work, particularly *Lulu*, techniques of set construction and set derivation manifest extreme complexity and orderliness (Perle 1985, Headlam 1985). Yet even his early, preserial pieces present complex techniques of aggregate construction and association (see Lambert 1993), manifesting compositional notions totally alien to tonal syntax.

on his use of established (Classic or Baroque) forms, and on quasi-tonal characteristics evident in surface melodic and harmonic patterns and by the construction of some of his sets (even more sophisticated recent approaches, e.g., Straus 1990, still deal almost exclusively with the accommodation of tonal pitch structures). My analysis, however, suggests that a different affinity is no less important: "gestural" similarity, here exhibited by similarity of contour-related configurations, of their relationships with other musical parameters, and of their structural and expressive roles.[25]

Berg's music clearly continues nineteenth-century Romanticism in the importance of melodic contour in delineating musical processes. Together with other "secondary" parameters (such as dynamics, textural density, and the rate of activity), melodic direction in Romantic music became consequential in defining processes of intensification and abatement.[26] Despite the entirely different procedures governing pitch structure in the bodies of music, Berg's use of contour clearly alludes to such nineteenth-century processes (whose structural significance is magnified because of the lack of supporting tonal implication). Recall, for example, the analysis of the *Adagio appassionato* of the *Lyric Suite* (Example 5.17), a movement whose succession of intensifying dynamic curves clearly constitutes an exaggerated, somewhat hysterical version of Wagnerian or Brucknerian processes (and indirectly of the periodic dynamic curves in earlier Romantic music, discussed in Chapter 4).

The impact of such processes in Berg stems not only from their "natural" directness (a result of reliance on melodic shape and other "secondary," non-syntactical parameters) but from the allusion to an alien musical language, from the sometimes bizarre combination of exaggerated nineteenth-century gestures, originally associated with tonal syntax, and an entirely different world of pitch organization. Thus, melodic contour in Berg serves not only structurally and emotively; combined with other strategies it points at the musical and cultural milieu from which Berg's expressivity stems.

25. This is not a resemblance to tonal music in general—Haydn's music, as we have seen, presents very different contour-related characteristics—but to nineteenth-century Romanticism in particular. See also Chapter 6.

26. See Agawu 1982, Hopkins 1990, Meyer 1989 (part III), and the Chopin analysis in Chapter 4.

CHAPTER 6

Conclusion: Style and Melodic Gesture

QUESTIONS

This chapter links and compares results in Haydn, Chopin, and Berg, to investigate whether the hypotheses of this study hold across styles. The investigation addresses several related but distinct questions.

To test my two principal hypotheses cross-stylistically, I examine whether all three samples present significant differences between peaks and controls (hypothesis 1), and particularly whether emphatic or intensifying features are cross-stylistically more frequent at peaks (hypothesis 2). I thus investigate whether peaks in all three styles are treated differently from other melodic phenomena, and specifically whether they feature cross-stylistic tendencies to associate with emphasis and intensification.

A more specific question is whether peaks are associated with the *same* features in all three styles. Which, if any, of the features studied here affect peaks regardless of the repertory examined? In other words, which of my secondary hypotheses regarding specific features are corroborated cross-stylistically?

A related issue is whether, with regard to each aspect examined, styles significantly differ at peaks. For instance, is there a statistically significant difference among styles concerning the association of peaks and syncopation? To address such questions adequately, it is not enough to compare the frequency of a feature at peaks in different styles; the results of such comparison may stem from the frequency of this feature in the general "population," rather than from any tendency specifically associated with peaks. For instance, peaks in Chopin may be syncopated more frequently than in Haydn simply because syncopation is more frequent in Chopin generally, at peaks or elsewhere. Hence, to inquire whether a tendency to associate *peaks* with a specific feature differs among styles, I compared, for each aspect, the peaks-controls ratios in the examined styles (using a three-dimensional chi-square analysis). The ratio between peaks and controls is a measure of the extent in which peaks are distinguished from other notes. A comparison of such ratios in different styles can, therefore, provide a measure of the differences between these styles concerning the extent in which peaks are set apart from other loci on the melodic curve.

Lastly, one may compare the three repertories globally, asking which repertory presents peaks more saliently. Determining the number of aspects for which results are statistically significant in each style is a simple way to address this question quantitatively.

STATISTICAL RESULTS

To aid addressing these questions, I present below three tables.

Table 6.1 summarizes the principal statistical results in the three bodies of music. For each aspect it presents the levels of significance (p) of results of peak-controls comparisons in the three styles, as indicated by chi-square or standard-score statistical tests. The table thus denotes whether, and to what degree, peaks and controls significantly differ in each aspect and for each style. For instance, in *metric location* the table shows that peaks and controls are not significantly different in Haydn ($p > .05$), suggesting that in this repertory peaks are not, as a rule, distinguished from other notes by metric location. In contrast, in both Chopin and Berg there is a significant difference between peaks and controls, that is, peaks are distinguished in both repertories with respect to meter. The level of significance, however, is higher in Berg ($p < .001$, vs. $p < .01$ in Chopin); that is, the tendency to distinguish peaks metrically seems to be stronger in that repertory.

In addition to results for the principal aspects (e.g., "metric location" or "approaching intervals") the table shows some noteworthy results for selected features. For instance, in addition to the results concerning the distribution of intervals as a whole, the table marks a tendency to use intervals larger than an octave at peaks in the Chopin and Berg repertories.

Table 6.2, which derives from Table 6.1, aims to facilitate stylistic comparison by concerning only aspects applicable to all three styles (excluding, for instance, "dynamics," which was not applicable to Haydn, or "harmonic degrees," not applicable to Berg), and presenting levels of significance graphically. Aspects in which peaks are significantly different from controls are marked by triangle (Δ) signs. The number of signs signifies the level of significance: Δ indicates a $p < .05$, $\Delta\Delta$ indicates $p < .01$, and $\Delta\Delta\Delta$ marks $p < .001$. Aspects in which no significant differences have been found ($p > .05$) are marked by a slash ($/$). The table also shows the number of aspects, in each style, for which results were statistically significant at the .05, .01, and .001 levels.

Table 6.3 presents the results of a comparison of the peaks-controls ratios in different samples.[1] As suggested above, this analysis provides, with regard to each

---

1. For the detailed data of this analysis, see Eitan 1991: 196–200. For a technical description of the analysis, see ibid., app. 9.

TABLE 6.1. Differences peaks/control: summary of statistical results

Aspect	Haydn	Chopin	Berg
DURATION AND METER			
Durational emphasis			
Relation with earlier neighbor	$p > .05$	$p < .01$ $(p < .001)^*$	$p < .001$
Relation with later neighbor	$p > .05$ $(p < .05)^*$	$p < .01$ $(p < .001)^*$	$p < .001$
Metric location	$p > .05$	$p < .01$	$p < .001$
1st beat (frequent at peaks)	$p > .05$	$p < .001$	$p < .0001$
Offbeats (infrequent at peaks)	$p > .05$	$p < .01$	$p < .0001$
Metric emphasis			
Relation with earlier neighbor	$p > .05$	$p < .001$	$p < .01$
Relation with later neighbor	$p > .05$ $(p < .05)^*$	$p > .05$ $(p < .05)^*$	$p < .05$
Syncopation	$p > .05$	$p > .05$	$p > .05$
Temporal Location			
Lower level	$p > .05$	$p > .05$	$p < .01$
3rd quarter	$p < .05$	$p > .05$	$p > .05$
4th quarter	$p > .05$	$p > .05$	$p < .01$
2nd half	$p > .05$	$p > .05$	$p < .0001$
Last note	$p > .05$	$p < .002$	$p < .001$
Middle level	$p > .05$†	$p < .01$	$p < .001$
1st quarter	$p > .05$	$p < .05$	$p < .001$‡
4th quarter	$p > .05$	$p < .01$	$p < .001$
2nd half	$p > .05$	$p < .01$	$p < .001$
Last note	$p > .05$	$p < .002$	$p < .001$
Higher level	$p > .05$	$p > .05$	$p < .01$
1st quarter	$p > .05$	$p > .05$	$p < .01$‡
4th quarter	$p > .05$	$p > .05$	$p < .01$
2nd half	$p > .05$	$p > .05$	$p < .005$

TABLE 6.1. Continued

Aspect	Haydn	Chopin	Berg
MELODIC RELATIONSHIPS			
Intervals			
Approaching	$p < .001$	$p < .0001$	$p < .001$
Disjunct	$p < .001$	$p < .001$	$p < .001$
Larger than a perfect fifth	$p < .001$	$p < .001$	$p < .001$
Perfect 4th	$p > .05$	$p < .05$	$p > .05$
Sixths	$p < .05$	$p < .001$	$p > .05$
Sevenths	$p > .05$	$p > .05$	$p < .01$
Octave	$p < .01$	$p > .05$	$p > .05$
Following	$p < .01$	$p > .05$	$p < .02$
Disjunct	$p < .01$	$p > .05$	$p > .05$
Larger than a perfect fifth	$p < .01$	$p > .05$	$p < .01$
Perfect fourth	$p < .05$	$p > .05$	$p > .05$
Sixth	$p < .05$	$p > .05$	$p > .05$
Octave	$p > .05$	$p < .01$	$p < .01$
Ascending	$p < .001$	$p < .001$	$p < .01$
Disjunct	$p < .001$	$p < .001$	$p < .002$
Larger than a perfect fifth	$p < .001$	$p < .001$	$p < .005$
Sixths	$p < .01$	$p < .01$	$p > .05$
Sevenths	$p > .05$	$p > .05$	$p < .05$
Octave	$p < .01$	$p > .05$	$p > .05$
>octave	$p > .05$	$p < .01$	$p > .05$
Descending	$p < .01$	$p > .05$	$p < .01$
Disjunct	$p < .001$	$p > .05$	$p < .05$
Larger than a perfect fifth	$p < .01$	$p < .05$	$p < .001$
Perfect fourth	$p < .002$	$p > .05$	$p > .05$
Larger than octave	$p > .05$	$p < .01$	$p < .002$
Melodic emphasis			
Relation with earlier neighbor	$p < .001$	$p < .0001$	$p < .001$
Relation with later neighbor	$p > .05$	$p < .005$	$p < .05$ $(p > .05)^*$
Scale-degree			
Local context	$p < .01$	$p > .05$	n.a.
$\hat{6}$	$p < .001$	$p > .05$	n.a.
$\hat{7}$	$p < .02$§	$p > .05$	n.a.
Principal tonality	$p > .05$	$p < .05$	n.a.
Repeated pitches	$p > .05$	$p < .05$§	$p > .05$

TABLE 6.1. Continued

Aspect	Haydn	Chopin	Berg
Pitch-register singularity			
In phrase	$p < .0001$	$p < .0001$	$p < .001$
In piece/movement	$p < .001$	$p < .0001$	$p < .001$
HARMONY			
Harmonic degrees	$p > .05$	$p > .05$	n.a.
Chord structure	$p < .01$	$p < .01$	n.a.
$\frac{6}{4}$ chords	$p < .001$	$p > .05$	n.a.
seventh chords	$p > .05$	$p < .001$§	n.a.
"Nontertial" verticalities	$p > .05$	$p < .05$	n.a.
Soprano positions	$p > .05$	$p < .01$	n.a.
Fifth	$p < .05$	$p > .05$	n.a.
Octave	$p < .05$§	$p < .05$	n.a.
Seventh	$p > .05$	$p < .01$§	n.a.
"Nonharmonic" tones	$p > .05$	$p < .05$	n.a.
DYNAMICS			
Dynamic emphasis			
Processive	n.a.	$p < .001$	$p < .001$
Local	n.a.	$p > .05$	$p > .05$
PARAMETRIC INTERACTION			
Combined parametric emphasis	$p > .05$	$p < .001$	$p < .001$
Interparametric congruence			
Meter-duration Peaks:	$p < .001$	$p < .05$	$p < .001$
Controls:	$p < .001$	$p < .001$	$p < .001$
Meter-melody Peaks:	$p > .05$	$p > .05$	$p < .01$
Controls:	$p > .05$	$p < .01$	$p > .05$
Duration-melody Peaks:	$p > .05$	$p > .05$	$p < .001$
Controls:	$p < .001$	$p < .001$	$p < .001$

*Parenthetical figures indicate results for H0: P(plus) = P(minus).
†For Haydn this is also the higher level (only two levels were examined in this repertory).
‡Peaks less frequent.
§Less frequent at peaks.

aspect, a measure of differences between styles concerning the extent in which peaks are differentiated from other notes. The column "all styles" (All) in the table compares peaks-controls ratios in all three samples. This comparison shows whether the treatment of peaks as "special points" is, with regard to the aspect investigated, style-dependent. The other columns, "Haydn-Chopin" (H-C), "Chopin-Berg" (C-B), and "Haydn-Berg" (H-B), present the results of similar comparisons between each two of the three samples. For instance, the column "all styles" indicates a significant ($p < .05$) stylistic difference in *metric location*, that is, it show that styles significantly differ in the extent in which they distinguish peaks metrically. The other columns pinpoint this difference, indicating that while Haydn significantly differs from both Chopin and Berg ($p < .05$), Chopin and Berg are not significantly different in this respect ($p > .05$). Results indicating significant stylistic differences are printed in this table in **bold** letters.

FINDINGS

1. Are the principal hypotheses cross-stylistically corroborated? The answer is a qualified yes for the first hypothesis, and a qualified no for the second. In each style investigated, peaks were distinguished from controls in some aspects (see Tables 6.1 and 6.2). Thus, peaks indeed are treated cross-stylistically as special points in the melodic curve, as postulated by the first principal hypothesis. However, few features tend to be associated with peaks in all three repertoires (see below), and some are peculiar to one repertory (e.g., the tendency to avoid second-inversion chords at peaks in Haydn, or the inclination to avoid successive repetitions of the peak note in Chopin). Further, the strength of the tendencies associated with peaks often differs considerably from one repertory to another (see Table 6.2).

The second principal hypothesis, postulating an association of peaks with emphatic or intensifying features, is corroborated for two of the three repertories, Chopin and Berg. In Haydn's music, few emphatic features are clearly related to peaks.

2. Are any specific tendencies related to peaks in all three styles? Two important tendencies are. Both involve melodic (as opposed to rhythmic or harmonic) features. First, in each style peaks tend to be approached (and to a certain degree left) by relatively large intervals, though no particular interval typifies approaches cross-stylistically (see "intervals" in Tables 6.1 and 6.2). Second, all three styles have a strong inclination to present the peak pitch only once in a segment. This tendency is particularly strong in relatively short segments (phrases, periods, or phrase groups), but it is also manifested in larger sections, though to a lesser degree (see "pitch-register singularity" in Tables 6.1 and 6.2).

These two findings are intriguing. They suggest that some tendencies concerning melodic shape transcend the boundaries of specific style and pitch syntax. They also suggest, however, that the most distinct of these cross-stylistic tendencies concern melodic contour per se, rather than its relationships with other musical domains.

TABLE 6.2. Style comparison

Aspect	Haydn	Chopin	Berg
Durational emphasis			
Earlier neighbor	/	ΔΔ	ΔΔΔ
Later neighbor	/	ΔΔ	ΔΔΔ
Metric location	/	ΔΔ	ΔΔΔ
Metric emphasis			
Earlier neighbor	/	ΔΔ	ΔΔΔ
Later neighbor	/	/	/
Syncopation	/	/	/
Temporal location			
Lower level	/	/	ΔΔ
Middle level	/	ΔΔ	ΔΔΔ
Higher level	/	/	ΔΔ
Intervals *			
Approaching	ΔΔΔ	ΔΔΔ	ΔΔΔ
Following	ΔΔ	/	Δ
Melodic emphasis			
Earlier neighbor	ΔΔΔ	ΔΔΔ	ΔΔΔ
Later neighbor	/	ΔΔ	Δ
Repeated pitches	/	Δ	/
Pitch-register singularity			
In phrase	ΔΔΔ	ΔΔΔ	ΔΔΔ
In piece/movement	ΔΔΔ	ΔΔΔ	ΔΔΔ
Combined parametric emphasis	/	ΔΔΔ	ΔΔΔ
Number of aspects where $p < .05$	5	12	14
Number of aspects where $p < .001$	4	6	9

*The aspects "ascending intervals" and "descending intervals" are not included in this table, as they are not independent of approaching and following intervals.

Do these inclinations represent some image of "good" melodic Gestalt, autonomous both from specific melodic idiom and from other musical aspects? Are they related in some way to cross-linguistic traits of speech intonation? Study of a wider repertory, including music outside the Western tradition, might answer these questions.

3. Which of the repertories are significantly different in handling melodic peaks, and which are alike? This issue is addressed, aspect by aspect, in Table 6.3. Unlike what might have been expected, the Berg and Chopin repertories, which are fundamentally different from each other in pitch organization, exhibit close similarity in the treatment of peaks, while the Haydn and Chopin repertories, alike in tonal syntax, differ considerably in handling peaks. In all but one aspect (pitch-register singu-

TABLE 6.3. Comparison of the ratios peaks-controls

Aspect	All	H–C	C–B	H–B
DURATION AND METER				
Durational emphasis				
Earlier neighbor	$p < .01$	$p > .05$	$p > .05$	$p < .001$
Later neighbor	$p < .02$	$p > .05$	$p > .05$	$p < .001$
Combined emphasis	$p > .05$	$.1 > p > .05$	$p > .05$	$p < .05$
Metric location	$p < .05$	$p < .05$	$p > .05$	$p < .05$
Metric emphasis				
Earlier neighbor	$p < .02$	$p < .05$	$p > .05$	$p < .01$
Later neighbor	$p > .05$	$p > .99$	$p > .05$	$p > .05$
Syncopation	$p > .05$	$p > .05$	$p > .05$	$p > .05$
Temporal location				
Lower level	$p > .05$	$p > .05$	$p > .05$	$p > .05$
Middle level	$p < .05$	$p > .05$	$p > .05$	$p < .01$
Higher level	$p > .05$	$p > .05$	$p > .05$	$p > .05$
MELODIC RELATIONSHIPS				
Intervals				
Approaching	$p > .05$	$p > .05$	$p > .05$	$p > .05$
Following	$p > .05$	$p > .05$	$p > .05$	$p > .05$
Melodic emphasis				
Earlier neighbor	$p > .05$	$p > .05$	$p > .98$	$p > .05$
Later neighbor	$p > .05$	$p > .05$	$p > .05$	$p > .05$
Scale-degree				
Local context	n.a.	$p > .05$	n.a.	n.a.
Principal tonality	n.a.	$p > .05$	n.a.	n.a.
Repeated pitches	$p > .05$	$p > .05$	$p > .05$	$p > .05$
Pitch-register singularity				
In phrase	$p < .02$	$p > .05$	$p < .05$	$p < .02$
In piece/movement	n.a.	n.a.	n.a.	n.a.
	(sample too small)			
HARMONY				
Harmonic degrees	n.a.	$p > .05$	n.a.	n.a.
Chord structure	n.a.	$p < .05$	n.a.	n.a.
Soprano positions	n.a.	$p < .02$	n.a.	n.a.
DYNAMICS				
Dynamic emphasis				
Processive	n.a.	n.a.	$p > .99$	n.a.
Local	n.a.	n.a.	$p > .95$	n.a.

Table 6.3. Continued

Aspect	All	H–C	C–B	H–B
PARAMETRIC INTERACTION				
Combined parametric emphasis				
Four degrees	$p < .05$	$p > .05$	$p > .05$	$p < .02$
Two degrees	$p < .02$	$p < .05$	$p > .05$	$p < .01$

larity),[2] there are no significant differences between Chopin and Berg, and in several aspects the similarity between the two repertories is striking, e.g., melodic emphasis ($p > .98$) and dynamic emphasis ($p > .99$). In contrast, in several important aspects (meter, duration, chord structure, soprano position, and, most important, combined emphasis) there are significant differences between the Chopin and Haydn repertories. Differences between Haydn and Berg are (not surprisingly) the most significant, and are present in most aspects.

What is surprising (at least if one defines styles in terms of pitch constraints) is that the differences between a tonal (Chopin) and a posttonal (Berg) repertory are minimal, while the differences between the two repertories sharing a tonal-functional syntax are considerable. The ramifications of this finding (to my mind, the most important finding of this study) will be discussed below.

4. Which repertory most decisively marks peaks for attention? As Table 6.2 indicates, peaks are most weakly associated with emphatic and intensifying features in the earliest repertory surveyed, and most strongly in the latest. In the Haydn sample such associations appear for only a few aspects and are not as a rule very significant; Chopin presents them in a stronger manner and in more aspects; and in the Berg sample the association of peaks with climactic and emphatic features is even stronger and featured by most domains. Thus, for instance, the tendency to emphasize peaks durationally is very weak in Haydn, stronger in Chopin, and strongest in Berg. A tendency to place peaks on strong beats (see "metric location" in Table 6.2), which is absent in the Haydn repertory, applies to both Chopin and Berg, but it is stronger in the latter. Similarly, the tendency to place peaks late in a segment (see "temporal location") is absent in the Haydn sample, in Chopin it applies to one level of segmentation, and in Berg it is exhibited at all levels of segmentation, up to entire pieces.

It is tempting to suggest that these results represent some kind of diachronic process, in which the importance of contour is intensified in line with changes in

2. Though a vast majority of peaks in the Berg sample (a larger majority than in the other two styles) appear once within their phrase group, that is also the case for a considerable minority of controls (see Table 5.11), probably because of serial constraints (and similar, though less formal constraints in the "free" posttonal music). Thus, the peaks-controls ratio is different in Berg than in the other two samples, though in all three the difference between peaks and controls is, in this respect, highly significant.

expressive norms (from eighteenth-century classicism, favoring expressive modera-tion and thus attenuating climax, through nineteenth-century romanticism, to early twentieth-century expressionistic idiom, intensifying Postromantic gestures). But of course, only a larger, more representative sample could validate a generalization.

DISCUSSION

Notwithstanding this study's strict limits in subject matter, musical repertory, and methodology, the results presented here are relevant to two broad issues. The first is the "nature versus nurture" controversy—the debate over the role of innate psycho-logical tendencies vis-à-vis learned cultural ones. The second concerns the interaction of pitch syntax with "gestural" dimensions of structure (such as melodic contour) in defining musical styles and style change.

Melodic Contour and Psychological "Nature" in Music

Pitch contour, and melodic peaks in particular, is a primeval feature of melody, inti-mately associated with innate psychological "nature." The emphatic and intensifying character of peaks is related to cross-cultural tendencies, featured, for instance, in the intonation of speech (see Chapter 1). A corroboration of my hypotheses in diverse musical repertories would suggest that these primitive, "natural," facets of melody are effective in Western music, regardless of specific melodic style and pitch syntax. It would thus strengthen a "naturalist" view, maintaining that innate psychological constraints and tendencies are important in shaping music even amid the complex of stylistic aptitudes, norms, and schemata characteristic of a musical repertory.

In support of this view, the diverse styles investigated here all treat peaks dif-ferently from other notes, suggesting that this "natural" emphatic phenomenon has influenced, regardless of style, the construction of musical pieces. Further, in some respects peaks are treated in all three styles in a way that enhances their "natural" emphatic status: the peak pitches often appear only once, and they are commonly surrounded by relatively large, emphasizing intervals. These results show at the very least that musics of diverse syntactical and expressive inclinations treat a conspicuous natural auditory phenomenon in a special manner (though not necessarily in exactly the same way), and thus that an aspect of "nature" has an effect on musical structure across styles.

In the main, however, this study suggests a more complex, more interesting view: the relation to "nature" and the treatment of the primitive aspects of sound-expression is itself an important facet of musical style. Indeed, diverse musical reper-tories all take account of conspicuous natural auditory features and their extramusical expressive implications (as the special treatment of peaks in all styles considered indicate). However, the degree to which such natural connotations are embodied in the style—whether they are strengthened or undermined—and their importance relative to the constraints of conventional musical syntax, may themselves be among the defining parameters of a musical idiom.

The increased importance of contour peaks in Chopin is a case in point. This change in the status of melodic shape may be part of a more general trend, the rise in significance of secondary parameters during the nineteenth century.[3] As Leonard B. Meyer suggests, this trend reflected a rise in the importance of "natural," as opposed to conventional, stipulations in nineteenth-century music. Meyer distinguishes "primary" parameters from "secondary" mainly by the capacity of the former (i.e., pitch, as measured in discrete intervallic relationships, and duration, as measured in proportional relationships) to produce discrete, proportional relationships among distinct elements, a capacity that makes them the principal carriers of musical syntax. "The primary parameters . . . are syntactic. That is, they establish explicit functional relationships (such as tonic and fifth, subdominant and dominant, accent and weak beat) and specific kinds of closure (authentic or deceptive cadences, masculine or feminine rhythms) that makes articulated hierarchies possible."[4] In contrast, secondary parameters are "statistical"—they create continuous processes, measured in degrees (higher-lower, louder-softer), rather than discrete relationships.[5] Because of the continuous and relative nature of the relationships statistical parameters create, discrete functional hierarchies and well-defined articulation and closure are less likely to emerge; in other words, it is difficult to establish a musical syntax based upon such parameters. Unlike primary parameters, governed chiefly by the learned conventions of musical syntax, secondary, "statistical" parameters—among them melodic contour—are controlled more by interstylistic, "natural" constraints. "Even in the absence of syntactic structuring, gradually rising pitches, increasingly loud dynamics, faster rates of motion, and a growth in the number of textural strands heighten excitement and intensity; while descending pitches, softer dynamics, slower rates of motion, and so on, lead toward relaxation, repose, and cessation" (Meyer 1989: 209).

The emphasis on rudimentary sonic dimensions, which are governed in part by their extramusical, "natural" connotations rather than by the conventions of a style-

3. This general tendency is indicated, among other things, by the increase in detail and frequency of notational signs marking dynamics, tempo, and timbre, and by the growing inclination to explore more extreme ranges of register and dynamics.

4. Meyer (1989): 209. See also pages 14–16, 208–211, 340–342, for discussions of the distinction between primary and secondary parameters, and of the role of secondary parameters in nineteenth- and twentieth-century music.

5. This distinction between "syntactical" and "statistical" parameters is not identical to the customary distinction between primary parameters (pitch and duration) and secondary (timbre and loudness). Rather, the same psychoacoustical parameter may have both syntactical and statistical dimensions. Pitch, for instance, which by way of proportional intervallic relationships serves as a basis for both tonal and nontonal (e.g., serial) grammars, also has two statistical dimensions: contour, defined by the continuum high-low, and the dimension of interval size as defined by the continuum of smaller and larger intervals. The interaction of these dimensions of pitch presents an important challenge to musical analysis.

specific musical syntax, is related to other aspects of Romantic musical style. These aspects may have themselves stemmed from ideological and sociological sources. First, the increased importance of secondary parameters compensated for the less direct, somewhat disguised presentation of conventional syntactical structures: the tendency to disguise cadential gestures (frequently veiled in Chopin by elaborate and sometimes idiosyncratic ornamentation) and stock tonal progressions (disguised in many of Chopin's pieces by extensive chromatic sequences and quasi-modal harmonic progressions) is thus balanced reliance on more direct, natural dimensions such as melodic shape. Such changes may themselves have been the result (probably unconscious) of the call of Romantic thinkers, from Rousseau onward, for a return to the "natural" in the arts, and the corresponding downgrading of "petty" convention and artifice. They might have also been a consequence of the lower level of musical sophistication of the new middle-class audience (Meyer 1989: 208–11).

In Berg, as we have observed, the inclination to highlight melodic shape is even stronger: in his reliance on this "natural" aspect of musical expression (as with other aspects of his musical rhetoric) Berg is a Romantic—indeed, a more obedient practitioner of the Romantic emphasis on the "natural" than most nineteenth-century composers. This tendency counteracts a compositional and precompositional framework that is, according to Berg himself, hardly perceptible (nor in need of perception) by the general audience,[6] and compensates for the absence of tonal directionality, by enhancing a dimension of structure and expression that is immediate in its impact, a dimension conveying emphasis and de-emphasis, intensification and abatement, without applying any specific pitch-syntax.[7]

Syntax and Gesture in Musical Style

The most thought-provoking finding of this study is the similar treatment of melodic peaks in the Chopin and Berg repertories, whose grammatical principles are entirely different, in particular the principles that underline their pitch organization. This finding is highlighted by the marked differences between the Haydn and Chopin repertories, which do have essentially the same pitch syntax. In other words, this study presents a stylistic break not between the tonal and posttonal repertories, not between repertories that supposedly use entirely different musical languages, but rather between repertories that use two dialects of the same tonal language.

One way to explain this incongruity is by separating the syntactic and formal di-

6. See, for instance, Berg's remark about *Wozzeck*: "there is no one in the audience who pays any attention to the various fugues, inventions, suites, sonata movements, variations and passacaglias—no one who heeds anything but the social problems of this opera" (quoted in Perle 1980: 531).

7. As in Romanticism, this important role of "natural" dimensions, such as contour, may be a conscious or unconscious result of an aesthetic approach. Berg believed strongly in the need to return to the sensual in the arts, a belief expressed early on in his well-known remarks on Wedekind's "new direction." See his letter of 18 November, 1907, quoted in Reich [1932] 1965: 22.

mensions of style from what may be called its "gestural" dimension. This dimension, expressed mainly through the "statistical," secondary parameters (such as melodic shape), is relatively independent of pitch syntax: styles that are similar in expressive gesture may be very different in their formal and syntactic bases, and vice versa. Thus, changes in musical style can be described differently when syntax, form, or gesture is the center. A syntactically radical style change can be a conservative continuation of an expressive, gestural path; and a clear continuation of a syntactical base can concur with a marked change in expressive gesture.

Meyer's distinction between the "syntactical" and "statistical" parameters is relevant here. The gestural dimension concerns mainly those aspects of musical style centered on the "natural," statistical parameters, such as melodic shape, attack rate, textural density, and dynamics. Because these parameters are relatively independent of the constraints of a specific musical syntax (though they often interact with it), expressive gestures based upon them can operate similarly in styles whose syntactic principles are different, for instance, in tonal and serial music.

How, for example, Berg's posttonal music (serial and "free") is related to other styles depends on whether musical relationships are viewed syntactically or gesturally. With regard to the grammar of pitch relationships few would hesitate to group Berg (the peculiarities of his treatment of the dodecaphonic premises notwithstanding) with Schönberg and Webern in one broad stylistic group. "Gesturally," however, Berg may have greater kinship with nineteenth-century Romanticism (and not only with late and Post-Romantic composers, but even with Chopin) than with Webern.

This similarity is exhibited by my statistical analysis and by the softer analyses of melodic shape that accompanied it. The statistics show a striking resemblance between Berg's work and a Romantic repertory with regard to many aspects of a local gesture—the configuration around contour peaks. The softer analysis indicates that this resemblance carries into longer-range and global strategies—for instance, the use of multi-level dynamic curves, the related tendency to place the highpoint (not only in the contoural sense) near the end of segments, and more specific strategies that accompany those markers of Romantic expression, such as intervallic and durational stretching.

My point is not that Berg's music retains some characteristics of nineteenth-century Romanticism (this observation has, of course, been made numerous times), but that this Romantic character is delineated in part by aspects of style that have little to do with the tonal syntax of nineteenth-century music, and that have not received the attention they merit. That such characteristics could be transformed from one style into another despite a radical change of "syntactic" base suggests the existence of an independent, nonsyntactic, gestural domain in music.[8]

8. Though relationships that are not "gestural" (for instance, the quasi-tonal construction of sets and the ensuing melodic and harmonic configurations) play a considerable role in shaping the Romantic character of Berg's music, I believe that his use of musical gesture (in the sense defined here) takes an important, and hitherto neglected, part in relating the music to nineteenth-century Romantic idioms. Thus,

For me, there are two reasons that make the study of gestural, nonsyntactic aspects of music potentially rewarding. One is that, because they are not dependent on a specific musical syntax, their study may shed light on commonalities between musical repertories that are remote in time and place. Such relations need not always be a result of historical influence or of a common cultural milieu (as the case seems to be in the repertories studied here) but might stem from a shared transcultural, "natural" source, combined with affinity in aesthetic approach and expressive tendencies. Further, the study of musical gesture may elucidate—perhaps better than a study of specific musical "grammars"—the relationships between musical discourse and extra-musical aspects of human expression.[9]

Second, "statistical" parameters of music—the principal domain of musical gesture as defined here—fall mostly in the sphere of tacit, unverbalized knowledge (to use Michael Polanyi's term). Missing are explicit rules, guidelines, and strategies, like those that have served for centuries as a basis for the instruction of musicians in tonal and modal syntax (recent endeavors, like those of total serialism or of composers in electroacoustic media, notwithstanding). As the present work makes evident, the reason for this disparity is not that the domain of musical gesture and of the "secondary," statistical parameters is too unsophisticated or marginal to be treated explicitly. Rather, the way in which musical gestures are used by composers and experienced by listeners may be inherently different from the way musical syntax and form are. An examination of the gestural dimension of music would, then, be an approach to a study of a different way of "thinking in music," perhaps more intimately related to embodied, "natural" tendencies than specific tonal grammars and formal designs. Such a study may eventually lead to a different way of thinking *about* music—to a different approach to the theory and analysis of an elusive realm of human expression.

---

the distinction between "gestural" and "syntactical" aspects of style may contribute to the on-going debate on Berg's place vis-à-vis Romanticism and Modernism (see, e.g., Pople 1993).

9. See Hatten 1993; Lidov 1990; Shove and Repp 1995, for discussions of gestural aspects of musical structures and their "extra-musical," kinesthetic connotations.

APPENDIX 1: PEAKS AND CONTROL NOTES EXAMINED

HAYDN

	Peaks		Controls	
	Measure	*Beat*	*Measure*	*Beat*

MINUETS FROM EARLY KEYBOARD SONATAS

	Measure	*Beat*	*Measure*	*Beat*
Sonata no. 1 in G, Hob. 16/8	5	2	4	1
	14	2	14	off 2/3
Sonata no. 2 in C, Hob. 16/7	6	1	5	off 2
	10	2	13	off 3
	22	off 1/2	22	off 1/2
	28	off 2	35	3
Sonata no. 3 in F, Hob. 16/9	6–7	off 3/1	1	1
	13	off 2	17	2
	29	3	31	2/3
	41	2	43	1
Sonata no. 4 in G, Hob. 16/G1	2	off 2	6	2
	16	off 2	15	3
	27	1	29	off 1
	35	off 3	33–34	2/1
Sonata no. 5 in G, Hob. 16/11	5	1	6	off 1
	11	3	14	1
	32	2	31	2
	40	3	50	3

Haydn Continued

	Peaks		Controls	
	Measure	*Beat*	*Measure*	*Beat*
Sonata no. 6 in C, Hob. 16/10	3	2	2off	3
	9	off 1	25	2
	33	off 1	29	2
	35	off 2	35	2
Sonata no. 7 in D, Hob. 17/D1	6	2	1	off 3
	13	2	3	1
Sonata no. 8 in A, Hob. 16/5	1	1	5 (B)	off 3
	9	1	13	off 3
	24	1	20	3
	28	3	31	2
Sonata no. 9 in D, Hob. 16/4	1	3	3	3/1
	11	2	13	off 3/
	28	off 3	25	off 3
	40	off 3	43	off 1
Sonata no. 10 in C, Hob. 16/1	3	3	5 (D)	off 3
	15	3	17 (G)	off 2
	21	off 1	22	3
	30	off 1	29	off 1
Sonata no. 11 in B flat, Hob. 16/2	1	off 3	12	2
	16	2	22 (C)	off 2
	35	3	31off	1
	51	3	42	off 2
Sonata no. 12 in A, Hob. 16/12	5	off 1	4	1
	21	2	19 (E)	off 1
	35	off 1	26	off 1
	48	off 2	43	off 2
Sonata no. 13 in G, Hob. 16/6	8	off 3	3	1
	11	1	13	off 2
	30	off 1	30	1
	46	off 2	53	2

HAYDN Continued

	Peaks		Controls	
	Measure	*Beat*	*Measure*	*Beat*
Sonata no. 14 in C, Hob. 16/3	3	3	8 (C)	off 1
	8	off 3	20 (B)	off 3
	24	3	30	2
	42	3	35	off 2
Sonata no. 15 in E, Hob. 16/13	4–5	off 3/1	3	off 2/3
	13	off 2/3	15–16	1
	25	off 1	30	off 3
	43	off 1	48	off 1
Sonata no. 16 in D, Hob. 16/14	5	off 2	7 (A)	off 1
	19	off 2	10 (G♯)	off 3
	34	off 1	36	1
	42	2	53	off 1
Sonata no. 17 in E flat, Hob. Deest	5	2	2	off 1 (F)
	21	2	24	off 2
	27	off 2/3	27	off 1/2
	47	off 2/3	46	off 3
Sonata no. 18 in E flat, Hob. Deest	3	2/3	5	2
	20	2	27	1
	38	off 1	36	off 3
	47	off 2	49	off 2

EARLY DRAMATIC PIECES

La Canterina: Intermezzo in Musica, Act I

Aria and recitative, "Che visino delicato"				
measures 1–40	32	off 2	31	off 2
measures 40–59	44	1	56	2
measures 60–78	62	off 4	61	off 4
measures 79–90	85	off 2	82–3	off 2/1

Recitative, "Decoro de' teatri"				
measures 91–102	92	3	92–3	3/2

HAYDN Continued

	Peaks		Controls	
	Measure	*Beat*	*Measure*	*Beat*
measures 103–146	118	off 2	141	1/off 2
measures 146–207	176	off 1	175	3/1
Accompanied recitative, "Che mai far deggio?"				
measures 1–39	31	off 2	31	3/off 3
measures 39–72	59	off 2/3	55	off 1/2
Aria, "Lo sposar l'empio tiranno"				
measures 1–71	54	3	32	1
measures 71–110	98	1	96	4
Accompanied recitative, "Che mai far deggio"				
measures 1–48	44	off 2/3	36	off 2
measures 49–74	61	1/2	56	off 2
measures 74–108	78	off 2	102	off 1
measures 108–143	109	off 2/3	123	off 1
measures 143–177	151	off 2	152	4
Quartet, "Scellerata"				
measures 1–48	43	3	39	off 3
measures 48–110	55	1	62	1
***La Canterina*, Act II**				
Recitative, "Uh, rovinate noi"				
measures 1—13	3	3	3	3
Aria, "Sinoir mio l'ufficio suo"				
measures 1–40	25	off 2	26	off 2
measures 41–61	41	off 1	47	1
Recitative, "Che mai vuol dir tal cosa"				
measures 1–40	22	1	35	3
Aria, "Non v'e chi mi aiuta"				
measures 1–48	16	1	12	1
measures 48–96	51	3	75	1

HAYDN Continued

	Peaks		Controls	
	Measure	*Beat*	*Measure*	*Beat*
Recitative, "Misera!"				
measures 1–29	24	off 4/1	19	3
measures 30–55	51	3	39	3/off 3
measures 55–71	61	3	68	3/o
Accompanied recitative, "O, stelle, aiuto"				
measures 1–19	5	3	17	off 1
measures 19–40	24–5	off 3/1	34	off 1
measures 38–63	46	off 2/3	47	off 2
Quartet, "Apri pur mia dea terrestre"				
measures 1–26	24	2	22	off 2
measures 26–66	37	off 2	51	off 1 (G)
measures 66–102	71	off 1	80	1
measures 102–149	135	off 2	139	off (B)
Acide				
Aria, "La beltà . . ."				
measures 1–43	29	off 3	29	2
measures 43–82	72	off 1	55	off 3
measures –116 (allegro)	96	3	90	3
Aria, "Perché stupisci"				
measures 1–49	38	1	18	off 1
measures 49–102	62	off 2	82	off 1 (B)
measures 102–134	129	1		
Aria, "Se men gentile"				
measures 1–61	29	off 1	39–44	off/1
measures 62–127	65	off 3	89	1
measures 128–156	136	1	129	off 2
Accompanied recitative, "Misero!"				
measures 1–22	4	off 3	11	3
measures 22–48	27	off 4/1	26–27	4/2
measures 48–69	55	2	49	off 4

HAYDN Continued

	Peaks			Controls	
	Measure	*Beat*		*Measure*	*Beat*
Aria, "Tergii vezzosi rai"					
measures 1–75	31	3		43	3
measures 75–148	88	1		118	off 1 (C)
measures 149–175	149	3		166	3
Quartet, "Ah vedrai"					
measures 1–92	36	off 2		69	off 1 (G♯)
measures 93–165	153	2		114	2/1

CHOPIN

	Peaks			Controls	
	Measure	*Beat*		*Measure*	*Beat*
MAZURKAS					
Opus 6 no. 1, in F♯ minor	13	1		12	2,3
	17	1		9	off 2
Opus 6 no. 2, in C♯ minor	9	off 1		7	off 1
	43 (appog.)	3		13	2
Opus 7 no. 1, in B♭ major	8	1		29	off 3
				24	1
Opus 7 no. 2, in A minor	21	1		46	off 1
	44	2, 3		3	off 1
Opus 17 no. 1, in B♭ major	15	1		34	3
	58	3		25	off 3
Opus 17 no. 2, in E minor	10	off 1		17	off 2
	26	3		36	3
Opus 24 no. 1, in G minor	4	1		20	2
	36	3		22	off 1

CHOPIN Continued

	Peaks		Controls	
	Measure	*Beat*	*Measure*	*Beat*
Opus 24 no. 2, in C major	25	1	13	3
	60	3	8	1,2
Opus 30 no. 1, in C minor	3	2	3	off 1
	36 (appog.)	1	42	1
Opus 30 no. 2, in B minor	2	off 1	2	off 2
	31	1	3	3
Opus 33 no. 1, in G♯ minor	4	off 1	3	off 3
	17	2	37	2
Opus 33 no. 2, in D major	1	off 3	22	off 3
	60	3	21	3
Opus 41 no. 1, in E minor	6	1	40	off 1
	33	2	29	off 3,1
Opus 41 no. 2, in B major	7	1	14	off 2
	54	1, 2	20	2
Opus 50 no. 1, in G major	4	1	3	2
	47 (l.h)	off 1	16	2
Opus 50 no. 2, in A♭ major	26	2	14	2
	67	1, 2	47	2
Opus 56 no. 1, in B major	16	3	13	2
	46	3	41	off 3,1
Opus 56 no. 2, in C major	13	3	26	off 1
	36	3	9	3
Opus 59 no. 1, in A minor	9	1	25	1
	55	2	10	1
Opus 59 no. 2, in A♭ major	12	3	2	3
	60	1	4	1

CHOPIN Continued

	Peaks		Controls	
	Measure	*Beat*	*Measure*	*Beat*
Opus 63 no. 1, in B major	11	1	7	1
	44	1	1	1
Opus 63 no. 2, in F minor	3	2	3	3
	34	3	2	1
Opus 67 no. 1, in G major	10	3	27	off 1
	29	2	12	2
Opus 67 no. 2, in G minor	14	off 2	7	2
	32	3	11	3
Opus 68 no. 1, in C major	10	off 3	7	2
	36	2	23[c]	1,2
Opus 68 no. 2, in A minor	8	1		
	31	2		
WALTZES				
Opus 18, in E♭ major	27	1	10–11	3,1
	87	3	23	1, off 3
	128	1	22	off 2
Opus 34 no. 1, in A♭ major	40	1	26	1
	73	off 1	44	3
	92	1	24	3
Opus 34 no. 2, in A minor	21	1	28	2
	66	off 1	24	off 2
	178 (left-hand)	1	46	2,3
Opus 34 no. 3, in F major	32	1	6	off 2, 3
	56	3	5	off 2,3
	103 (appog.)	1	30	off 3

CHOPIN Continued

	Peaks		Controls	
	Measure	*Beat*	*Measure*	*Beat*
Opus 42, in A♭ major	25	off 2	43	2
	46	3	56	off 3
	164off	2/3	61	2
Opus 64 no. 1, in D♭ major	32	off 3	7	off 3
	50	1	7	3
			26	off 3
Opus 64 no. 2, in C♯ minor	13	off 2,3	39	3
	48	1	35	3
	75	3	22	1
Opus 64 no. 3, in A♭ major	13	2	27	off 2
	103 (left-hand)	2	16	2
	156	off 3	19	2
Opus 69 no. 1, in A♭ major	9	2	19	off 2,3
	18	1	37	off 2,3
	56	1	29	off 2,3
Opus 69 no. 2, in B minor	13	1	37	off 3,1
	31	3	33	2
	53	2, 3	46	2
Opus 70 no. 1, in G♭ major	10	1	5	off 3
	28	1	33	off 2,3
			33	off 3,1
Opus 70 no. 2, in A♭ major	13	1	3	1
	48	1	5	off 2
			14	3
Opus 70 no. 3, in D♭ major	7	off 2	3	1
	36 (l.h.)	1	20	off 3,1
	50–51	3, 1	45	1

CHOPIN Continued

	Peaks		Controls	
	Measure	Beat	Measure	Beat
KK IVa #12, in E major	29	3	50	3
	69	1	10	1
KK IVa #13, in A♭ major	16	1	18	1
	43	3	24	off 2
			2	2
KK IVa #15, in E minor	33	off 3	3	off 1
	60	1	39	2
KK IVb #10, in E♭ major	14	3	9	off 3,1
	23	1	8	off 3
KK IVb #11, in A minor	23	2,off 3	12	1
	33	off 2	7	3

BERG

	Peaks			Controls		
Segment	Measure	Beat		Measure	Pitch	Beat

Lyrische Suite für streichquartet

1st Movement

Segment	Measure	Beat	Measure	Pitch	Beat
1–12	12	1 (2/4)	3	E♭5	off 2
13–22	20	2 (2/4)	16	D5	off 1
23–35 (1–35)	27	2	26	A4	off 1
36–48	48	1	41	B♭4	1
53–61 (36–69)	53	2	53	F7	3
62–69	67	off 4	62	E4	off 2

2nd Movement

Segment	Measure	Beat	Measure	Pitch	Beat
1–15 (1–80)	13	1	2	G♯5	3 (6/8)
16–40	39	off 3	36	B4	off 2
41–55	49	4	41	C7	1

BERG Continued

	Peaks			Controls		
Segment	Measure	Beat		Measure	Pitch	Beat
56–80	72	off 1		68	G^5	off 2
81–91	91	1		83	D♭^{4}	off 4
91–104	96	1		101	F♯^{4} (v.2)	3
105–142	116	1/3		105	A^5	3
143–150	147	4/5		144	C^5	off 1
3rd Movement						
1–69	67	off 2		9	E♭^{5}	3
70–92	92	1		85	B^4	off 6
92–138	95	2		103	D^7	off 1
4th Movement						
1–14	13	3		9	B^3	off 3
14–23	22	off 1		18	F♯^{5}	off 2
23–44	39	3		31	B♭^{5}	off 3
45–58	53–56			51	A^3	off 3/
59–69	68	1/3		62	B♭^{4}	off 3
5th Movement						
1–50	8	3		45	A♭^{7}	1
51–120	111	1		62	B♭^{4}	1
121–211	170	1		148	F^4	2
212–325	302	1		267	B♭^{4} (v.2)	1
326–440	398	3		409	G^2	13
441–460	445	2		453	A^5	1
6th Movement						
1–16	8	1		6	B♭^{5} (v.2)	off 3
17–36	30	off 3		29	B♭^{5}	off 2
36–46	42	off 3		35	B^5	3
Vier Stucke für klarinette und klavier						
I	8	1		1	B^4	off 2
II	5	1		7	E^3	off 4
III	13	1		6	F♯^{2}	3
IV	16	off 4		8	C^5	2

BERG Continued

Segment	Peaks			Controls		
	Measure	Beat		Measure	Pitch	Beat

Der Wein: Konzertarie für Sopran

Die Seele des Weines

1–23	21	4	20	G♯^{4}	off 4
23–30	27	off 2	25	F♯^{4}	off 2
31–72	35	off 4	35	G^2	3
73–87	81	off 2	76	A^4	off 2/3

Der Wein der Liebenden

88–111	108	4 (6/4)	93	D^5	4
112–172	136	3 (3/4)	121	G^4	3

Der Wein des Einsamen

173–195	176	4	184	D♭^{5}	2
195–216	207	2 (4/4)	197	D♯^{5}	off 1

Lulu: Oper in Drei Akten nach dem Tagödien
Erdgeist und *Buchse der Pandora* von Frank Wedkind

Prolog	55	1	25	A^3	off 4

1st Act, 1st Scene

Rec.	102	2 (3/4)	100	B♭^{4}	2/off
Intro.	141	2 (4/4)	139	E♭^{4}	off 2
Canon	168	off 1	179	E♭^{5}	off 1
Coda	195	off 1/2	187	B^4	off 1
Canzon.	276	off 6	276	C^5	2
Rec.	295	off 1	287	F♯^{4}	off 2
Duet	318	off 2	312	A^4	off 3
Arioso	349	off 2	332	D♭^{4}	3

1st Act, 2nd Scene

Duettino	427	2	440	E^5	1/2
Cham.I	484	1/off 3	519	E♭^{4}	off 2
Son/Exp	557	2 (6/8)	562	D^5	off 2
Son/Rep	666	1	652	D^5	off 2
Monor.(I)	735	1	737	A♭^{3}	off 2

BERG Continued

	Peaks			Controls		
Segment	Measure	Beat		Measure	Pitch	Beat
1st Act, 3rd Scene						
Andante	1036	off 4/1		1039	G$\flat$5	1
Eng. Wal.	1073	3		1075	F4	off 2
Rec.	1098	1		1097	E$\flat$5	off 1
Choral	1145	3 (3/4)		1125	A$\flat$3	off 2
Ragtime	1167	1		1171	E$\flat$5	2/1
Sextet	1190	off 3		1189	A5	off 4
Son/Dev	1277	4 (6/4)		1255	D5	3/4
3rd rep	1332	off 1		1303	F4	off5
2nd Act, 1st Scene						
Rec.	21	off 2		25	C5	2
Ballade	52	3		51	A3	off 1
Cavat.	70	off 3		66	D5	off 4
Langs.	164	1		156	D5	1/3
Canon	190	off 2		190	D5	5
Ensamble	223	1		202	E$\flat$5	3
225–74	265	off 4		230	D$\flat$2	3
275–94	279	4		279	G4	off 3
295–310	303	off 4		302	E$\flat$4	off 3
317–37	330	off 3		330	G5	
338–79	350	1		350	B3	off 1
Dr. Sch.	435	2/3		478	A3	off 1
Lied L.	532	1		504	E5	off 2
Tumult	562	3		565	A5	1
Arietta	647	1		642	F$\sharp$5	3
2nd Act, 2nd Scene						
Rec.	760	1		751	F5	off 1
Larg/rec	818	2/off 2		810	D$\flat$2	3
Chamb.	903	2		846	F$\sharp$4	off 3
1000–58	1010	1		1019	F$\sharp$5	off 1
1057–97	1084	2		1085	F$\sharp$5	off 1
Hymn	1142	1		1131	A3	off 3

APPENDIX 2: RANDOM NUMBERS (1–200) USED TO DETERMINE CONTROLS

Ia. Haydn (sonatas)

Sequential #	Random #	Sequential #	Random #	Sequential #	Random #
1	89	24	176	47	15
2	98	25	77	48	138
3	162	26	111	49	108
4	128	27	50	50	133
5	61	28	14	51	143
6	109	29	186	52	98
7	105	30	72	53	138
8	111	31	88	54	29
9	164	32	129	55	66
10	190	33	128	56	87
11	147	34	45	57	130
12	143	35	127	58	8
13	173	36	175	59	45
14	5	37	63	60	193
15	85	38	43	61	145
16	75	39	199	62	57
17	120	40	179	63	36
18	170	41	79	64	140
19	82	42	187	65	83
20	85	43	90	66	187
21	86	44	155	67	62
22	47	45	160	68	17
23	134	46	9		

Ib. Haydn (operas)

Sequential #	Random #	Sequential #	Random #	Sequential #	Random #
1	189	33	58	65	113
2	56	34	102	66	142
3	6	35	81	67	28
4	156	36	59	68	85
5	49	37	13	69	26
6	161	38	88	70	159
7	121	39	99	71	170
8	195	40	23	72	61
9	121	41	199	73	104
10	90	42	74	74	149
11	135	43	69	75	106
12	175	44	16	76	46
13	17	45	191	77	37
14	108	46	75	78	185
15	50	47	47	79	159
16	38	48	156	80	139
17	72	49	198	81	96
18	105	50	130	82	32
19	173	51	57	83	115
20	9	52	194	84	167
21	38	53	168	85	39
22	164	54	34	86	194
23	69	55	94	87	63
24	167	56	35	88	90
25	23	57	112	89	16
26	121	58	195	90	196
27	74	59	53	91	3
28	78	60	38	92	168
29	142	61	118		
30	82	62	187		
31	31	63	151		
32	158	64	70		

II. CHOPIN

Sequential #	Random #	Sequential #	Random #	Sequential #	Random #
1	38	35	24	69	9
2	105	36	69	70	15
3	97	37	9	71	13
4	90	38	156	72	135
5	86	39	77	73	116
6	169	40	121	74	110
7	105	41	165	75	142
8	80	42	10	76	109
9	176	43	30	77	55
10	12	44	30	78	91
11	9	45	17	79	58
12	149	46	188	80	11
13	90	47	47	81	40
14	172	48	31	82	193
15	189	49	154	83	48
16	41	50	38	84	156
17	40	51	65	85	85
18	146	52	48	86	25
19	157	53	34	87	119
20	133	54	63	88	37
21	77	55	127	89	6
22	137	56	98	90	10
23	129	57	173	91	199
24	77	58	9	92	181
25	90	59	140	93	115
26	179	60	104	94	109
27	141	61	70	95	144
28	161	62	156	96	65
29	142	63	72	97	31
30	195	64	87	98	49
31	34	65	61	99	91
32	183	66	33	100	121
33	185	67	13		
34	9	68	176		

III. BERG

Sequential #	Random #	Sequential #	Random #	Sequential #	Random #
1	9	35	154	69	22
2	18	36	147	70	172
3	82	37	167	71	200
4	100	38	172	72	168
5	197	39	62	73	122
6	90	40	169	74	73
7	4	41	120	75	98
8	158	42	97	76	183
9	54	43	18	77	38
10	197	44	17	78	198
11	73	45	49	79	73
12	18	46	66	80	174
13	195	47	28	81	191
14	2	48	13	82	187
15	7	49	10	83	7
16	75	50	103	84	61
17	76	51	4	85	50
18	87	52	122	86	27
19	164	53	8	87	12
20	190	54	163	88	46
21	154	55	4	89	170
22	101	56	194	90	118
23	164	57	93	91	95
24	140	58	88	92	37
25	56	59	19	93	50
26	132	60	97	94	58
27	182	61	162	95	71
28	153	62	129	96	120
29	95	63	106	97	71
30	127	64	144	98	145
31	151	65	164	99	32
32	198	66	90	100	195
33	115	67	142		
34	6	68	191		

WORKS CITED

Adams, Charles R. 1976. "Melodic Contour Typology." *Ethnomusicology* 20: 179–215.

Agawu, V. Kofi. 1982. "The Structural Highpoint as Determinant of Form in Nineteenth Century Music." Ph.D. dissertation, Stanford University.

———. 1983. "On Schubert's 'Der Greise Kopf'." *In Theory Only* 8/1: 3–21.

———. 1984. "Structural 'Highpoints' in Schumann's *Dichterliebe*." *Music Analysis* 3/2: 159–80.

Attneave, Fred. 1954. "Some Informational Aspects of Visual Perception." *Psychological Review* 61: 183–93.

Attneave, Fred and R. K. Olson. 1971. "Pitch as a Medium." *American Journal of Psychology* 84: 147–66.

Bach, C. P. E. [1762] 1949. *Essay on the True Art of Playing Keyboard Instruments*. Translated by W. J. Mitchell. New York: Norton.

Baker, M. A. and M. Loeb. 1973. "Implications of Measurements of Eye Fixations for a Psychophysics of Form Perception." *Perception and Psychophysics* 13: 185–92.

Benjamin, William E. 1984. "A Theory of Musical Meter." *Music Perception* 1: 355–413.

Berry, Wallace. 1976. *Structural Functions in Music*. Englewood Cliffs, N.J.: Prentice-Hall.

———. 1985. "Metric and Rhythmic Articulation in Music." *Music Theory Spectrum* 7: 7–33.

Bingham, W. Van Dyke. 1910. "Studies in Melody." *Psychological Review; Monograph Supplements XII /3*: 1–88

Bolinger, Dwight L. 1958. "A Theory of Pitch Accent in English." *Word* 14: 109–49.

———. 1985. "The Inherent Iconism of Intonation." in John Haiman, ed., *Iconicity In Syntax: Proceedings of a Symposium on Iconicity in Syntax, Stanford, June 24–26, 1983*. Vol. 6 of *Typological Studies in Language*, a companion to the journal *Studies in Language*. Amsterdam and Philadelphia: John Benjamins: 97–108.

———. 1986. *Intonation and Its Parts*. Stanford, Calif.: Stanford University Press.

Boltz, M. and Mari Riess Jones. 1986. "Does Rule Recursion Make Melodies Easier to Reproduce? If Not, What Does?" *Cognitive Psychology* 18: 389–431.

Bregman, Albert S. 1990. *Auditory Scene Analysis: The Perceptual Organization of Sound.* Cambridge, Mass.: MIT Press.

Bregman, Albert S. and J. Campbell. 1971. "Primary Auditory Stream Segregation and Perception of Order in Rapid Sequences of Tones." *Journal of Experimental Psychology* 89: 244–49.

Brown, A. Peter. 1986. *Joseph Haydn's Keyboard Music: Style and Sources.* Bloomington: Indiana University Press.

Carlsen, James C. 1981. "Some Factors Which Influence Melodic Expectancy." *Psychomusicology* 1: 12–29.

Carlson, Rolf, Y. Erikson, B. Granström, B. Lindblom, and K. Rapp. 1975. "Neutral and Emphatic Stress Patterns in Swedish." In G. Fant, ed., *Speech Communication: Proceedings of the Speech Communication Seminar, Stockholm* Vol. 2. Stockholm: Almqvist and Wiksell International.

Carlson, Rolf, A. Friberg, L. Fryden, B. Granström, and J. Sundberg. 1989. "Speech and Music Performance: Parallels and Contrasts." *Contemporary Music Review* 4: 391–404.

Clynes, Manfred and E. Nettheim. 1982. "The Living Quality of Music." In Manfred Clynes. ed., *Music, Mind and Brain: The Neurobiology of Music.* New York: Plenum Press.

Cogan, Robert. 1984. *New Images of Musical Sound.* Cambridge, Mass. and London: Harvard University Press.

Cogan, Robert and Pozzi Escot. 1976. *Sonic Design: The Nature of Sound and Music.* Englewood Cliffs, N.J.: Prentice-Hall.

Cohen, Dalia. 1971. "Palestrina Counterpoint: A Musical Expression of Unexcited Speech." *Journal of Music Theory* 15: 99–111

———. 1983. "Birdcalls and the Rules of Palestrina Counterpoint: Towards the Discovery of Universal Qualities in Vocal Expression." *Israel Studies in Musicology* 3: 96–123.

Cooper, Grosvernor and Leonard B. Meyer. 1960. *The Rhythmic Structure of Music.* Chicago: University of Chicago Press.

Cooper, W. E., C. Soars, A. Ham, and K. Damon. 1983. "The Influence of Inter- and Intraspeaker Tempo on Fundamental Frequency and Palatalization." *Journal of the Acoustical Society of America* 73: 1723–30.

Cruttenden, Alan. 1986. *Intonation.* Cambridge: Cambridge University Press.

Deliege, Irene. 1987. "Grouping Conditions in Listening to Music: An Approach to Lerdahl and Jackendoff's Grouping Preference Rules." *Music Perception* 4/4: 325–59.

Deutsch, Diana. 1978. "The Psychology of Music." In E. C. Carterette and M. P. Friedman, eds., *Handbook of Perception*, Vol. 10. New York: Academic Press: 191–218.

DeWitt, L. A. and R. G. Crowder. 1986. "Recognition of Novel Melodies After Brief Delays." *Music Perception* 3: 259–74.

Divenyi, P. L. and I. J. Hirsh. 1978. "Some Figural Properties of Auditory Patterns." *Journal of the Acoustical Society of America* 64: 1369–86.

Dowling, W. Jay. 1978. "Scale and Contour: Two Components of a Theory of Memory for Melodies." *Psychological Review* 85/7: 341–54.

———. 1982. "Melodic Information Processing and Its Development." In Diana Deutsch, ed., *The Psychology of Music*. New York: Academic Press: 413–30.

———. 1994. "Melodic Contour in Hearing and Remembering Melodies." In Rita Aiello, ed., *Musical Perceptions*. New York and Oxford: Oxford University Press: 173–90.

Dowling, W. Jay. and D. S. Fujitani. 1971. "Contour, Interval, and Pitch Recognition in Memory for Melodies." *Journal of the Acoustical Society* 49: 524–31.

Dowling, W. Jay. and D. L. Harwood. 1985. *Music Cognition*. London: Academic Press.

Drake, Carolyn, W. Jay Dowling, and Caroline Palmer. 1991. "Accent Structures in the Reproduction of Simple Tunes by Children and Adult Pianists." *Music Perception* 8/3: 315–34.

Drake, Carolyn and Caroline Palmer. 1993. "Accent Structures in Music Performance." *Music Perception* 10/3: 343–78.

Edworthy, Judy. 1985. "Melodic Contour and Musical Structure." In Peter Howell, Ian Cross, and Robert West, eds., *Musical Structure and Cognition*. London: Academic Press: 169–87.

Eitan, Zohar. 1991. "Style and Gesture: A Study of Melodic Peaks." Ph.D dissertation, University of Pennsylvania.

———. 1995. "Beethoven's Thematization of Musical Space: The Case of the *Appassionata*." *Sonus* 16/1: 22–55.

———. 1997. "Registral Direction and Melodic Implication." Paper presented to the 16th Congress of the International Musicological Society, London.

Fletcher, Harvey. 1953. *Speech and Sound in Communication*. New York.: Van Nostrand.

Fonagy, Ivan and Klara Magdics. 1972. "Emotional Patterns in Intonation and Music." In Dwight Bollinger, ed., *Intonation*. London: Penguin.

Friberg, Anders. 1991. "Generative Rules for Music Performance: A Formal Description of a Rule System." *Computer Music Journal* 15: 56–71.

Friedmann, Michael. 1985. "A Methodology for the Discussion of Contour: Its Application to Schoenberg's Music." *Journal of Music Theory* 29: 223–48.

———. 1987. "A Response: My Contour, Their Contour." *Journal of Music Theory* 31: 268–74

Garner, W. R. and R. L. Gottwald. 1986. "The Perception and Learning of Temporal Patterns (Part 2)." *Quarterly Journal of Experimental Psychology* 20: 97–109.

Gjerdingen, Robert O. 1988. *A Classic Turn of Phrase: Music and the Psychology of Convention*. Philadelphia: University of Pennsylvania Press.

Hart, Johan 't., R. Collier, and A. Cohen. 1990. *A Perceptual Study of Intonation: An Experimental-Phonetic Approach to Speech Melody.* Cambridge: Cambridge University Press.

Hasty, Christopher. 1997. *Meter as Rhythm.* Oxford: Oxford University Press.

Hatten, Robert. 1993. "Schubert the Pregressive: The Role of Resonance and Gesture in the Piano Sonata in A, D. 959." *Integral* 7: 38–81.

Headlam, Dave. 1985. "The Derivation of Rows in *Lulu.*" *Perspectives of New Music* 24/2: 198–233.

Heise, G. A. and G. A. Miller. 1951. "An Experimental Study of Auditory Patterns." *American Journal of Psychology* 64: 68–77.

Hopkins, Robert G. 1990. *Closure in Mahler's Music: The Role of Secondary Parameters.* Philadelphia: University of Pennsylvania Press.

Hulse, Stewart H., A. H. Takeuchi, and R. F. Braaten. 1992. "Perceptual Invariances in the Comparative Psychology of Music." *Music Perception* 10/2: 151–84.

Huron, David. 1990a. "Increment/Decrement Asymmetries in Polyphonic Sonorities." *Music Perception* 7/4: 385–94.

———. 1990b. "Crescendo/Diminuendo Asymmetries in Beethoven's Piano Sonatas." *Music Perception* 7/4: 395–402.

———. 1996. "The Melodic Arch in Western Folksongs." *Computing in Musicology* 10: 3–23.

Huron, David and Matthew Royal. 1996. "What Is Melodic Accent? Converging Evidence from Musical Practice." *Music Perception* 13/4: 489–516.

Jarman, Douglas. 1979. *The Music of Alban Berg.* London: Faber.

Jeppesen, Knud. 1927. *The Style of Palestrina and the Dissonance.* Oxford: Oxford University Press.

———. 1939. *Counterpoint: The Polyphonic Vocal Style of the Sixteenth Century.* Englewood Cliffs, N.J.: Prentice-Hall.

Jones, Mari Riess. 1987. "Dynamic Pattern Structure in Music: Recent Theory and Research." *Perception and Psychophysics* 41/6: 631–34.

Jones, Mari Riess, M. Boltz, and G. Kidd. 1982. "Controlled Attending as a Function of Melodic and Temporal Context." *Perception and Psychophysics* 32/3: 211–18.

Koch, Heinrich. 1802. *Musicalisches Lexikon.* Frankfurt am Main.

Kolinski, Mieczyslaw. 1965. "The Structure of Melodic Movement: A New Method of Analysis." *Studies in Ethnomusicology* 2: 96–120.

———. 1966. "The General Direction of Melodic Movement." *Ethnomusicology* 9: 240–64.

Kramer, Jonathan D. 1985. "Studies of Time and Music: A Bibliography." *Music Theory Spectrum* 7: 98–104.

Krumhansl, Carol L. 1990. *Cognitive Foundations of Musical Pitch.* Oxford: Oxford University Press.

Lakoff, George and Mark Johnson. 1980. *Metaphors We Live By.* Chicago: University of Chicago Press.

Lambert, Philip. 1993. "Berg's Path to Twelve-Note Composition: Aggregate Construction and Association in the Chamber Concerto." *Music Analysis* 12: 321–42.

Landon, H. C. Robbins. 1978. *Haydn: Chronicle and Works*. Vol 2. London: Thames and Hudson.

Landon, H. C. Robbins and David Wyn Jory. 1988. *Haydn: His Life and Music*. Bloomington: Indiana University Press.

Larsen, Jans Peter. 1980. "Haydn, Joseph." In Stanley Sadie, ed., *The New Grove Dictionary of Music and Musicians*, vol. 8. London: Macmillan.

Larson, Steve. 1993. "Modeling Melodic Expectation: Using Three 'Musical Forces' to Predict Melodic Continuations." *Proceedings of the Fifteenth Annual Conference of the Cognitive Science Society*: 629–34.

Lerdahl, Fred and Ray Jackendoff. 1983. *A Generative Theory of Tonal Music*. Cambridge, Mass.: MIT Press.

Lidov, David. 1987. "Mind and Body in Music." *Semiotica* 66/1: 69–97.

Lieberman, P. and S. B. Michaels. 1962. "Some Aspects of Fundamental Frequency and Envelope Amplitude as Related to the Emotional Content of Speech." *Journal of the Acoustical Society of America* 34: 922–27.

Lussy, Mathis. 1874. *Traité de l'expression musicale*. Paris.

Marvin, Elizabeth West and Paul A. Laprade. 1987. "Relating Musical Contours: Extensions of a Theory for Contour." *Journal of Music Theory* 31: 225–67.

Mattheson, Johann. [1739] 1981. *Der Vollkommene Capellmeister*. Tran. E. C. Harris. Ann Arbor, Mich.: UMI Research Press.

Mehler, J., J. Bertoncini, M. Barriere, and D. Jassik-Gerschenfeld. 1978. "Infant Recognition of Mother's Voice." *Perception* 7: 491–97.

Meyer, Leonard B. 1956. *Emotion and Meaning in Music*. Chicago: University of Chicago Press.

———. 1973. *Explaining Music: Essays and Explorations*. Chicago: University of Chicago Press.

———. 1980. "Exploiting Limits: Creation, Archetypes, and Style Change." *Daedalus* 109/2: 177–205.

———. 1989. *Style and Music: Theory, History, and Ideology*. Philadelphia: University of Pennsylvania Press.

Monahan, C. B. and E. C. Carterette. 1985. "Pitch and Duration as Determinants of Musical Space." *Music Perception* 3/1: 1–32.

Monahan C. B., R. A. Kendall, and E. C. Carterette. 1987. "The Effect of Melodic and Temporal Contour on Recognition Memory for Pitch Change." *Perception and Psychophysics* 41/6: 576–600.

Morris, Robert D. 1987. *Composition with Pitch-Classes: A Theory of Compositional Design*. New Haven, Conn. and London: Yale University Press.

———. 1993. "New Directions in the Theory and Analysis of Musical Contour." *Music Theory Spectrum* 15/2: 205–28.

Nakamura, A. 1987. "The Communication of Dynamics Between Musicans and Listeners Through Musical Performance." *Perception and Psychophysics* 41/6: 525–33

Narmour, Eugene. 1977. *Beyond Schenckerism: The Need for Alternatives in Music Analysis*. Chicago: University of Chicago Press.

———. 1989. "The 'Genetic Code' of Melody: Cognitive Structures Generated by the Implication-Realization Model." *Contemporary Music Review* 4: 45–63.

———. 1990. *The Analysis and Cognition of Basic Melodic Structures: The Implication-Realization Model*. Chicago: University of Chicago Press.

———. 1992. *The Analysis and Cognition of Melodic Complexity*. Chicago: University of Chicago Press.

O'Connor, J. P. and G. F. Arnold. 1961. *Intonation of Colloquial English*. London: Longman.

Ortmann, O. 1926. "On the Melodic Relativity of Tones." *Psychological Monographs*: 1–35.

———. 1937. "Interval Frequency as a Determinant of Melodic Style." *Peabody Bulletin* 12: 3–10.

Oster, Ernst. 1961. "Register and the Large-Scale Connection." *Journal of Music Theory* 5: 55–71.

Perle, George. 1980. "Berg, Alban." In Stanley Sadie, ed., *The New Grove Dictionary of Music and Musicians*, vol. 2. London: Macmillan: 524–38.

———. 1985. *The Operas of Alban Berg*. Vol. 2, *Lulu*. Berkeley and Los Angeles: University of California Press.

Polansky, Larry, and Richard Bassein. 1992. "Possible and Impossible Melody: Some Formal Aspects of Contour." *Journal of Music Theory* 36: 259–84.

Pople, Anthony. 1993. "Secret Programmes: Themes and Techniques in Recent Berg Scholarship." *Music Analysis* 12/3: 381–99.

Ratner, Leonard G. 1982. *Classic Music: Expression, Form and Style*. New York: Schirmer Books.

———. 1984. *Music, the Listener's Art*. Berkeley and Los Angeles: University of California Press.

———. 1992. *Romantic Music: Sound and Syntax*. New York: Schirmer Books.

Reich, Willi. [1937] 1965. *Alban Berg*. London: Thames and Hudson.

Riemann, Hugo. 1884. *Musicalische Dynamik und Agogic: Lehrbuch der Musikalischen Phrasierung*. Hamburg.

Rosen, Charles and Henry Zerner. 1979. "The Permanent Revolution." *New York Review of Books* 26/17: 23–30.

Rosner, Burton. L. and Leonard B. Meyer. 1986. "The Perceptual Roles of Melodic Process, Contour and Form." *Music Perception* 4/1: 1–39.

Rousseau, Jean-Jacques. [1758] 1969. *Dictionnaire de musique*. Hildesheim and New York: Georg Olms.

Samson, Jim. 1985. *The Music of Chopin*. London: Routledge and Kegan Paul.

Sedlacek, K. and A. Sychra. 1963. "Die Melodie als Factior des Emotionellen Ausdrrucks." *Folia Phoniatrica* 15: 89–98.

Seeger, Charles. 1960. "On the Moods of a Music Logic." *Journal of the American Musicological Society* 13: 224–61.

Sheer, Miriam. 1989. "The Role of Dynamics in Beethoven's Instrumental Music." Ph.D. dissertation, Bar Ilan University (Ramat-Gan, Israel).

Shepard, R. N. 1982. "Structural Representations of Musical Pitch." In Diana Deutsch, ed., *The Psychology of Music*. New York: Academic Press: 344–99.

Shove, Patrick and Bruno H. Repp. 1995. "Musical Motion and Performance: Theoretical and Empirical Perspectives." In John Rink, ed., *The Practice of Performance: Studies in Musical Interpretation*. Cambridge: Cambridge University Press: 55–83.

Sloboda, John A. 1992. "Empirical Studies of Emotional Response to Music." In Mari Riess Jones and Susan Holleran, eds. *Cognitive Bases of Musical Communication*. Washington, D.C.: American Psychological Association. 33–46.

Straus, Joseph. 1990. *Remaking the Past: Musical Modernism and the Influence of the Tonal Tradition*. Cambridge, Mass. and London: Harvard University Press.

Sundberg, Johan. 1982. "Speech, Song, and Emotions." In Manfred Clynes, ed., *Music, Mind and Brain: The Neurobiology of Music*. New York: Plenum.

Sundberg, Johan, A. Friberg, and L. Fryden. 1991. "Threshold and Preference Quantities of Rules for Music Performance." *Music Perception* 9/1: 71–92.

Thomassen, J. M. 1982. "Melodic Accent: Experiments and a Tentative Model." *Journal of the Acoustical Society of America*. 71/6: 1596–1605.

Toch, Ernst. 1948. *The Shaping Forces of Music*. New York: Dover.

Trehub, S. E. 1987. "Infants' Perception of Musical Patterns." *Perception and Psychophysics* 41: 635–41.

Trehub, S. E., D. Bull, and L. A. Thorpe. 1984. "Infants' Perception of Melodies: The Role of Melodic Contour." *Child Development* 55: 821–30.

Türk, Daniel Gottlieb. 1789. *Klavierschule*. Leipzig.

Vos, Piet G. and Jim M. Troost. 1989. "Ascending and Descending Melodic Intervals: Statistical Findings and Their Perceptual Relevance." *Music Perception* 6/4: 383–96.

Wagner, Richard. [1850] 1965. "Das Kunstwerk der Zukunft" (selections). Translated by Oliver Strunk. In Oliver Strunk, ed., *Source Readings in Music History: The Romantic Era*. New York: Norton: 136–63.

Watkins, Anthony J., and Mary C. Dyson. 1985. "On the Perceptual Organization of Tone Sequences and Melodies." In Peter Howell, Ian Cross, and Robert West, eds., *Musical Structure and Cognition*. London: Academic Press: 71–119.

Watt, Henry J. 1923. "Functions of the Size of Interval in the Songs of Schubert and of the Chippena and Teton Sioux Indians." *British Journal of Psychology* 14: 370–86.

Watson, C. S. and W. J. Kelly. 1981. "The Role of Stimulus Uncertainty in the Discrimination of Auditory Patterns." In D. J. Getty and J. H. Howard, eds., *Auditory and Visual Pattern Recognition*. Hillsdale, N.J.: Erlbaum.

Weinberger, Norman M. and Thomas M. McCenna. 1988. "Sensitivity of Single Neurons in the Auditory Cortex to Contour: Toward a Neurophisiology of Music Perception." *Music Perception* 5/4: 355–90.

Williams, C. E. and K. N. Stevens. 1972. "Emotion and Speech: Some Acoustical Correlates." *Journal of the Acoustical Society of America* 52: 1238–50.

Williams, David B. 1990. "Effects of Selected Music Factors on Second- and Fifth-Grade Children's Perception of Melodic Motion." *Psychomusicology* 9/1: 59–78.

Woodrow, H. A. 1951. "Time Perception." In Stanley Smith Stevens, ed., *Handbook of Experimental Psychology*. New York: Wiley: 1224–36.

Wright, Anthony A. et al. 1985. "Memory Processing of Serial Lists by Pigeons, Monkeys and People." *Science* 229: 287–89.

Zarlino, Gioseffo. [1558] 1986. *Le institutioni harmoniche*. Trans. G. Marco and C. Palisca. New Haven, Conn.: Yale University Press.

Name Index

Subject Index

Accent. *See* Emphasis

Appoggiaturas. *See* Harmony: non-harmonic tones

Bilinear melody, 43–44, 64, 125, 129n

Cadence. *See* Closure; Pre-cadential schema; Pre-cadential peak

Chord structure. *See* Harmony

Classic style, 14–15, 33–34, 45, 149. See also *Galant* idioms

Climax, 3–4, 45, 51–53, 61, 62 (Example 4.3), 63, 70, 86, 88, 100, 113, 115, 132–33, 138–39. *See also* Dynamic curve; Structural highpoint

Closure, 45, 70, 88, 100, 103, 137, 150–51. *See also* Pre-cadential schema; Pre-cadential peak; Terminal fall

Dynamic curve, 3–4, 9–10, 40, 55, 61–63 (Example 4.3), 81 (Example 4.10), 83–84, 98n, 100, 121–25 (Example 5.17), 138, 139, 153. *See also* Intensification-abatement model

Dynamics, 62 (Examples 4.3), 84, 115, 118 (Example 5.17), 139, 152; dynamic emphasis (aspect in analysis), 13–14, 25, 61, 78–79 (Examples 4.8, 4.9), 83, 86, 90 (Example 5.2), 133, 134 (Example 5.21), 137, 144, 147

Emotional expression, 2, 3, 5, 10–11, 83–84, 103, 115, 151, 152; in speech intonation, 2, 5, 10–11. *See also* Text setting

Emphasis, 2, 5–8, 51–53, 83–84, 137, 149; combined (*see* Parametric interaction); durational (agogic, aspect in analysis) 9, 20, 21 (Example 2.2) 29, 30 (Example 2.8), 34–35, 36–39 (Examples 3.1–3.7), 55–56, 57–58 (Examples 4.1–4.2), 56, 83, 86, 87–95 (Examples 5.1–5.5), 104 (Example 5.8), 118, 142, 146, 147, 148, 149; dynamic (*see* Dynamics); emphasis versus accent (Mattheson) 3–4 (Example 1.1); grammatical versus rhetorical 7–8, 12–13

(Example 1.2), 76–78, 103; metric (*see* Meter); melodic (aspect in analysis), 10–11, 23, 30 (Example 2.8), 31–32, 36–38 (Examples 3.1–3.4, 3.7), 41, 66–68, 83, 101–2, 143, 145–48 (*see also* Intervals); in speech intonation 4–5, 13; trochaic versus iambic accent (Riemann) 40n. *See also* Hypotheses, principal

Expressionism, 133n, 149

Form, conventional, 17, 52, 63n, 138–39, 152, 154

Galant idioms, 33, 52–53

Gap-fill schema, 30 (Example 2.8), 45, 57 (Example 4.1), 69, 81 (Example 4.10), 83, 86, 90 (Example 5.2), 103–12 (Examples 5.9–5.13), 138

Genre (effect on results), 33–34, 54–55, 84

Gestalt principles, 17, 148

Gesture versus syntax (as aspects of style), 14–16, 84, 87–88, 103–12, 138–39, 148–49, 152–54. *See also* Secondary parameters

Harmony, 2, 12–13 (Example 1.2), 24–25, 30 (Example 2.8), 47–49, 61, 74–78, 80n, 83, 109–10, 112 (Example 5.13), 144, 147, 150–51; and "grammatical" versus "rhetorical" emphasis, 12–13 (Example 1.2), 70–73 (Example 4.6); chord structure (aspect in analysis), 24–25, 31–32, 48, 74–75, 144, 145–46, 147 (seventh chords), 75–77 (Example 4.7), 144; second inversion triads, 48–49 (Example 3.13), 53, 74–75, 144; non-harmonic tones, 18 (Example 2.1), 58 (Example 4.2), 74, 76–78, 83, 144); modulation, 70–72 (Example 4.6); scale degrees, harmonic (aspect in analysis), 24, 29–30, 48, 61–62 (Example 4.3), 71–73 (Example 4.6), 74, 77, 144, 147; soprano position (aspect in analysis), 25, 31–32, 48–49, 144, 147, 148

Hierarchy of peaks, 98–100, 112, 153. *See also* Nested configurations